WINRUNNER
IN SIMPLE STEPS

WINRUNNER
IN SIMPLE STEPS

by

Hakeem Shittu

WinRunner in Simple Steps

Copyright © 2007 by Hakeem Shittu.

ISBN: 978-0-6151-5289-9

Trademarked names may appear in this book. Rather than use a trademark symbol with every occurrence of a trademarked name, we use the names only in an editorial fashion and to the benefit of the trademark owner, with no intention of infringement of the trademark.

Copy Editor: Abraham Simon
Cover Design Consultant: Tayo Faleye

For information on translations, please contact the authors directly at info@genixpress.com, or visit http://www.genixpress.com.

The information in this book is distributed on an "as is" basis, without warranty. Although every precaution has been taken in the preparation of this work, neither the author(s) nor Genixpress shall have any liability to any person or entity with respect to any loss or damage caused or alleged to be caused directly or indirectly by the information contained in this work.

CONTENTS

AUTHOR PROFILE

Hakeem Shittu is a computer geek who spends his time shared between doing real work (consulting, training and conferences) and playing with a host of technologies and platforms. He's slightly obsessed with Tivos and is working on a black belt in Photoshop-fu. You can contact Hakeem through his software company, Gen!x Inc., at hshittu@genixcorp.com.

ACKNOWLEDGEMENTS

I would like to thank everyone that helped bring this project to fruition.

David Simon, who conceived this project and nurtured it to realization.

Abraham Simon, without whom this project would have languished in development for much longer.

Bella, for being so *purr*fect.

PREFACE

Software testing is an important part of the application development process, but unfortunately, it is most often ignored until the last moment. Or sometimes, it is left to the programmers to adequately build and test the system. It is not a surprise therefore that a large majority of software application projects fail.

With appropriate planning and testing, there is no reason why high quality applications cannot be delivered to clients. This book seeks to reduce the perceived difficulty of testing complex GUI and web applications by introducing WinRunner, an automated testing tool for Windows application.

What Do I Need to Use This Book?

This book is aimed at seasoned and entry-level software testers with an interest in testing and test automation. The best value of this book is for those interested in doing test automation with Mercury's WinRunner product.

I have provided a background in this book for users that might be very new to the process of testing by describing the software development process. Where possible, the information is generalized enough to be useful with most automated testing tool. Keep in mind however, that Mercury's WinRunner is the major focus of the book and all the code snippets provided will work only with WinRunner.

I have provided several useful examples in this book and included complete information about the software application that we will be testing in the book.

The book is broken up into the following sections:

Chapter 1: Introduction To Testing – You are introduced to the process of software development in the form of the Software Development Life Cycle (SDLC). Emphasis is placed on the testing phase of the SDLC.

Chapter 2: Automated Testing – You learn the difference between manual and automated testing. The processes of both automated and manual testing are described and the benefits of automated testing are highlighted.

Chapter 3: Important Concepts In Test Automation – You discover the different software concepts that must be considered for automating tests including types of applications that can be tested in WinRunner, recording and playback, add-in architecture and object recognition.

Chapter 4: Introducing WinRunner – You are introduced to WinRunner and how to launch and use the application. The many sub-tools provided by WinRunner are also introduced and extensively described.

Chapter 5: Using WinRunner – You learn about the process of performing automated testing using WinRunner. You also learn about the software application that will be used in this book for examples.

Chapter 6: Mapping The GUI – You acquire the skills to create a GUI Map file. You learn about the different tools that are provided to create this file and how to use them in modifying and deleting the object references contained within the file.

Chapter 7: Recording A Test – You learn how to create a test using the record/playback feature of WinRunner. You are introduced to the different recording modes and how to choose the correct mode for your test case.

Chapter 8: Working With Tests – You discover what you do with your test after recording your test case including such items as adding comments. You also learn about the different files created on your filesystem by WinRunner.

Chapter 9: Enhancing A Test – You acquire the skills to enhance your test with test artifacts that are useful in verifying properties and functionalities. The test artifacts covered in this chapter include synchronization points and data parameterization.

Chapter 10: Checkpoints – You learn more about test enhancement with the use of checkpoints. The different checkpoints available in WinRunner are presented and how to use each of them in your test is discussed.

Chapter 11: Test Script Language – You explore the features of the script language built into WinRunner and learn how to create and modify test scripts using this language.

Chapter 12: Putting It All Together – You get the chance to utilize the material covered thus far in creating several test cases. This is in tune with the book's hands-on approach.

Chapter 13: Running & Debugging Tests – You manage the execution of test cases that you have created and learn how to search for, and resolve, any problems that are found in these test cases.

Chapter 14: Analyzing Results – You explore the tests results viewer and how to get detailed information about different types of operations that may be included in your test script.

Chapter 15: Batch Test – You discover how to use the powerful batch test facility in WinRunner to group several tests and execute them in a series.

Chapter 16: RapidTest Script Wizard – You discover a great tool that can be used to jump start the creation of GUI Map files and test scripts. You learn the many handy features of the RapidTest Script Wizard tool.

CONTACTING THE AUTHOR

Feel free to send me feedback or ask me questions. My e-mail address is hakeem@genixpress.com. Please visit the Gen!x Press website at http://www.genixpress.com for information about this book as well as my upcoming books.

BEFORE WE BEGIN

This book is designed to be a hands-on introduction with the greatest benefits derived by following along with the projects and exercises for this you will find the following details useful:

Directory - All the examples in this book use a root directory named C:\MyTests. You may wish to create a similar folder on your machine to follow along.

Test Download – You may download all the tests we create in this book from http://www.genixpress.com/gp/files/wiss.zip.

Software – Mercury provides a trial version of WinRunner that you can download from http://www.mercury.com.

CHAPTER 1

INTRODUCTION TO TESTING

"Testing is the process of exercising or evaluating a system or system component by manual or automated means to verify that it satisfies specified requirements, or to identify differences between expected and actual results."

- Institute of Electrical and Electronics Engineers (IEEE).

Software applications have grown in recent years from simple console based applications that perform a single task. Now they are complex, visually pleasingly and animated programs that perform a variety of difficult tasks. It is no longer unusual for a single application to perform complex tasks, integrate with many other applications as well as multiple back-end systems, and process documents in a variety of formats. An example of this is online banking.

The features available in these software applications have substantially advanced out of a need to support a more sophisticated and computer savvy user base. In addition to this, today's users have many more choices of computing devices such as PCs, laptops, PDAs, Tablet PCs, smartphones, Pocket PCs etc. Also a great variety of operating system choices are available for these devices and all of these systems require software to be developed for performing various tasks.

The need for testing these software applications is therefore very clear because testing helps to ensure that applications developed meet with the original intent of the customer. The complexity that applications must support today comes at a price to developers because each of the many features being created have to be tested in multiple scenarios and different environments to ensure that they work properly as intended. And in the event that the user performs an invalid operation, the system should generate a meaningful message to the user about why the failure occurred.

It is not unusual to download and use an application and find that an attempt to do something impossible, like save a document directly to a CDROM drive, will cause the application to crash. This is because the developer of the application did not foresee the multiple scenarios that end-users of the application would attempt while using the application. While the end-user might be wrong to save a document to a read-only drive, it is still important for the application to recover from the scenario gracefully without causing the user to lose the work done to their document.

This is precisely why we do software testing. It provides the ability to rigorously test a software application to ensure that the application meets with the originating requirements and expectations. Testing also helps to ensure that the application continues to function even when used in unintended ways. If problems are found during the development phase of an application, they can be fixed before the application is made available to end-users.

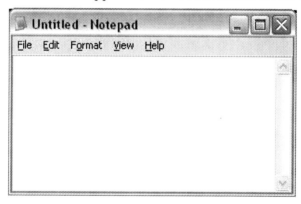

Figure 1.1: The Windows Notepad application.

This directly impacts the cost of development. You may be familiar with the 1:10:100 rule of testing which states that the cost to fix a defect increases exponentially the longer it takes to identify the defect. Testing thereby helps ensure that the end-user is provided with a quality product and an error-free experience.

An example of the exponential growth in application features can be seen in document editing software. Notepad, a standard application shipped with all versions of Microsoft Windows and shown in Figure 1.1, is a simple text editor capable of editing text documents.

NOTE: The notepad application is accessible from Start ▶ Programs ▶ Accessories ▶ Notepad

---

For a long time, Notepad has been the standard for quick document editing exercises in the Windows environment. It is rapidly losing its dominant place to a host of new tools that provide more advanced features that are useful while editing text documents. Textpad (www.textpad.com) shown in Figure 1.2 is an example of the new generation of text editors. It is a versatile document editing application that can be used to edit documents of many formats providing such useful features as formatting, multiple document view and syntax highlighting.

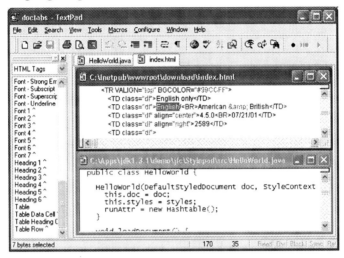

Figure 1.2: The Textpad application.

In Figure 1.2 Textpad is shown editing both a HTML and Java document in two windows. Notice that it provides syntax highlighting features to these different file formats.

Developers of editing tools such as this would need to put the application through a rigorous process to test all these advanced features.

Software Development Life Cycle

The development of software applications is based on a lifecycle process known as the software development lifecycle (SDLC). SDLC is a software engineering process that provides information about steps that need to be taken to advance a software project from concept to deployment. SDLC is broken into 5 phases with each phase dependent upon results from the preceding phase. Each phase also specifies what must happen during that portion of the software process. The testing process, which we are primarily concerned with in this book, is the fourth phase in the SDLC process.

SDLC helps describe an approach which, when followed properly, ensures that applications meet both the functional and visual requirements

3

stipulated in their creation documents. The phases contained within the SDLC process include:

Requirements Analysis Phase – In this phase, the Business Analysts (BA) will gather details about what needs to be done, and how the application should perform those tasks. The Business Analysts (BA) must meet with all the stakeholders in the application to capture all the needs and details of what they want the application to do. The most difficult part of this process is ensuring that the requirements are:

Complete – containing all necessary functionalities needed by the users.

Non-conflicting – Often with a large user base it is easy to have a group of users need a feature that conflicts with features needed by other users. This must be negotiated during this stage because the application cannot be built with conflicting requirements.

Unambiguous – written in clear language so that the same meaning can be derived when different parties read the document.

The result of this process is determining the features that must exist in the final application.

Design Phase – This phase is managed by a software architecture team that will create the high-level design of the application. The high-level design is a blue-print that specifies how the application will be created. It takes into consideration the programming language and software platform in which the application will be developed. These details will determine how the internal structure of the application will be designed. Additional activities during this phase includes the creation of flowcharts that describe how components within the application will interact, designing the screen layout that dictate what the application would look like, and also creating the database structures that the application might use to store data.

Implementation and Unit Testing Phase – This phase involves writing the code for the application using the chosen programming language and software platform from the design phase. A software application being created in the Java programming language for instance might be coded using the Abstract Windowing Toolkit (AWT), or Java Foundation Classes (JFC) or even the Standard Widget Toolkit (SWT) for the object library. The choice of the tool to use is made during the design phase, and the implementation would simply create the application conforming to this decision. The choice of interface technology determines the actual type of software code that the developer will write. During this process, unit testing is performed at the code level to ensure the correctness of the software functions that are created by the programmer. Unit testing also ensures the several functions can work together in completing tasks.

Testing Phase – The testing phase covers the process of planning tests that will be executed to examine the application's functionality, performance, usability etc. The phase also describes how the test would the execution of these tests. Decisions are made about using a manual or automated approach and test cases are created based on the chosen test strategy. During this phase, the goal is to test the entire application to ensure that when all the separate components that make up the application are assembled, the application functions as described in the requirements documents.

Maintenance – On completion and release of an application, there is often a need for corrective maintenance to handle defects that were undiscovered in the development process, and preventive maintenance to mitigate issues that might arise from external threats. Additionally there is often a desire to upgrade certain functionality for the application. For deployed applications such as your bank's web application, there is also a need to support to users and manage configurations of the software system. The maintenance cycle describes how this process should be handled.

From the above, you may notice that the SDLC process is originally intended to be a linear process with one phase completing before the commencement of the next. You must have requirements before you know how to design your database structure, and likewise you need this database structure to know what tables and fields to use in your programming code.

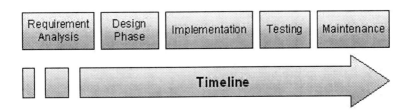

Figure 1.3: SDLC Timeline.

Figure 1.3 shows the SDLC process implemented linearly. However, as time is always a major factor in software development with many companies seeking to reduce the time-to-market for new products, methodologies have been created to optimize SDLC by allowing certain parts of it to function in parallel. These methodologies are processes designed to maximize the efficiency of the SDLC. Some of these methodologies include Scrum, Agile, Extreme Programming (XP) and the Rational Unified Process (RUP). The underlying goal of each of these methodologies are to optimize the software development timeline while ensuring the quality of the resulting product.

By staggering the starting time of the subsequent phases, it is often possible to achieve a level of parallel development. As shown in Figure 1.4, this has a net effect of saving the project time by having multiple things done simultaneously. Note that the difference in the methodology being used will impact how the phases are staggered.

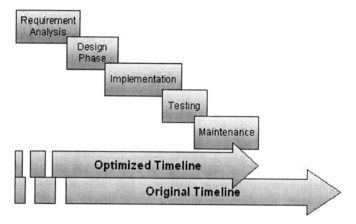

Figure 1.4: Optimized SDLC Timeline showing concurrent phases.

ASK THE EXPERTS

Q: Should the functional tester understand the programming language with which the application was created?

A: Understanding the programming language is not necessary. During functional testing we are only exposed to the completed application and not to the source code. Functional testing ignores the internal mechanisms of an application and focuses on the output provided for a given input.

Q: What is the best software development methodology?

A: This question is analogous to asking "what is the best programming language?" Each methodology has its strong suit and expectedly its weaknesses. All of them however, seek to make it easier for a project to be completed successfully on-schedule, and on-budget.

SDLC Testing Phase

The testing phase as a part of the SDLC process governs the preparation for testing, the management of testing resources and the creation of test cases. It also manages the execution of these tests as well as the creation and tracking of defects found within the software application.

Although there is less consensus about the phases of the software testing process than there is about the SDLC process, you can generally find that the testing software systems is broken down in to the following phases:

Test Planning - The goal of this phase is to create a process that specifies the details as well as the logistics involved with the testing process. It takes into account the tools that will be used to test the application, the testing environment etc. Usually, a test plan document results from this phase, describing in details such crucial items as:

- Roles and responsibilities of everyone involved in the testing process
- Process of setting up the test environment
- Obtaining and managing test data
- Standards for test creation and execution
- Preliminary schedule for testing
- Test management process
- The defect-tracking process
- Software tools that would be used through the testing process

Test Design - Involves the breakdown of the functional and performance requirements for the application into a series of test cases. These test cases are documents that describe how a specific functionality is going to be tested. In order to successfully test any functionality, it is important that the test case completely identifies what needs to be done. Also, the test case needs to specify the sequential process that needs to be followed, any results expected and include all other relevant pieces of information. Table 1.1 contains a list of useful information that would be found in a test case.

Item	Description
Test Name	The name that would be given to the test script. This would allow a correlation between the test case that describes what is being tested and the test script that performs the test.

Purpose	The feature that is being tested.
Pre-Condition	The initial condition that must be met for the feature being tested to be properly tested.
User action	A sequential step-wise listing of actions that the user is expected to perform in order to appropriately test the desired functionality.
Expected result of each action	The result that is expected after each action performed by the user.
Post-Condition	The condition in which the test environment should be returned to on the completion of this test.
Valid Test Data	Source and location where valid test data can be found to test the functionality being tested. This data will be either hard-coded into the test script, or preferably, entered into the data table and parameterized into the test
Possible Exceptions	List of possible exceptions that can occur during this test. This information is used for creating recovery scenarios.

Table 1.1: Useful data needed in a test case.

I have provided below in Listing 1.1, a test case that contains all these useful information. You should note that using tools such as Mercury's TestDirector, it is easy to capture and track this crucial information.

Test Name:
```
Add Expense
```

Purpose:
```
Verify that when expense records are added they display
within the application and are added to the database
```

Pre-Conditon:
```
None
```

Step	User Action	Expected Result
1	Launch the AUT	
2	Click the Today's Date button	Correct system date appears in the available textbox
3	Enter in additional details for an expense	

		record
4	Click the save button	a. Expense is displayed in the grid. b. Totals' textbox is updated. c. Expense record is saved to database
5	Close the AUT	

```
Post-Condition:
      None.

Valid Test Data:
      Category: Movies
      Description: LOTR Return of the King at Lennox
      Amount: 11.50
```

Listing 1.1: Add Expense Test Case.

Test Development - This phase is only necessary for software applications that will be tested using automated software testing tools. In this phase, the test cases created in the previous stage, are converted into executable scripts. These scripts will then be executed using an automated testing tool. This step is unnecessary for applications that are being manually tested because manual testing involves the performance of the contents in the test case by individuals.

I will talk more about manual vs. automated testing in the next chapter.

Summary

In this chapter you have learned:

- What software testing is, and why we test software applications.

- The software development lifecycle, and where testing fits into this process.

- How to shorten the software development lifecycle by making certain phases run concurrently.

- The different parts of the software testing process.

CHAPTER 2

AUTOMATED TESTING

As I have mentioned in the previous chapter, testing can be done through manually performing actions on an application just like an end user would or performing these actions through the use of automated testing tools. In this chapter I will talk about the process involved in manual testing and contrast that to automated testing. You probably already suspect that automated testing has several benefits over manual testing. That is correct. I will discuss these benefits in this chapter and also introduce the family of testing tools provided by Mercury Interactive (www.mercuryinteractive.com) for use in automated testing.

Testing Types

There are two choices available to you while testing your software application and these are:

- Manual Testing: Performed by a tester who carries out actions on the tested application manually and compares the result of each step to results specified in the requirements document..

- Automated Testing: Automation of the manual process (as described above) using software tools for test execution.

In the manual process of software testing, a tester performs tests on an application by replicating the same processes that an end user will perform. The steps to replicate are often specified in a test case document such as the one provided in Listing 1.1. The tester then uses visual and logical checks to verify that the functionality in the systems matches up with what is required in the test case. If the task can be completed as described with all the expected results noted in the test case meeting with the actual result found during the testing process, the test is said to have passed. If not, a defect is said to exist in the application and appropriate steps would be taken to document the defect and provide the information to the application developers to fix the problem.

NOTE: A defect in a software application is generally referred to as a bug in the application.

Manual testing is mostly used for console-based applications, which traditionally have much fewer concurrent sub-processes running. Often these applications do not have a wide degree of variability based on input i.e. they are often created to manage a single task (or a rather limited number of tasks) so the amount of test cases that will be created for them will be small. By contrast, Graphical User Interface (GUI) applications often run with multiple threads executing. This creates longer test cases and therefore difficulty in appropriately executing all test steps properly.

Manual testing is also used in software applications that require improvisation during the testing process. These applications, such as video games cannot be automated because of the randomness of response that is required by the user during the application runtime.

You may begin to see that *structure* is a key feature that is required for automated testing. Automated testing is structural in nature and uses a scripting language to commit to file the manual actions a user performs on an application. The automated testing tool in use is said to record the user action. Execution of this test script simply replays the operations the user performed on the application. This process is known as playback. In addition to the recorded operations, the tester adds checks and conditional statements into the test script to verify specific features within the application.

The automated testing tool also provides additional advantage over the manual human tester such as the ability to gather more detailed information about the software system than an individual can. For instance, a requirement specification that details that all buttons be 24 pixels in height cannot easily be verified through manual testing but can be found easily through automated testing.

The Benefits of Automated Testing

While manual testing requires only access to the application being tested, it is much slower than automated testing and lacks the ability to be scheduled and executed round-the-clock. Automated tests, when written properly do not have this limitation. They can be scheduled to run simultaneously on several machines through nights, weekends and holidays. This makes a lot of difference on a project with a compact schedule. Automated testing requires the use of additional tools to create an automated testing script as well as execute these scripts. It additionally requires individuals skilled in the use of these tools. The cost of both of these items is often seen as a barrier for smaller firms and projects to use automated testing tools. For firms that are able to take the plunge however, automated testing provides significant benefits over its manual counterpart. Some of these include.

- Test execution is significantly faster when automated than what can be accomplished by a human tester manually.

- Execution of the test is consistent and can be repeatedly under the same set of conditions eliminating the possibility of error being made by a tester being marked as a defect. This also makes it easier to determine when a defect has been fixed in an application

- Test scripts can be reused, with little or no modifications, to test features in later versions of the same software application.

- Automated testing tools provide detailed results of the test execution process, which can help the developer identify any problems quicker.

- Allows better usage of tester time and resources. Automated tests would allow, for instance, a tester to create test scripts and manage defects during the day while running the automated test unattended overnight.

- Eases the task of comprehensively testing the application by allowing multiple scenarios of the same feature to be easily tested.

- Uses programming extensions to extract important information from the application and the computer system that may not be easily available when using the manual testing approach.

- Follows a well-documented approach that allows all defects in an application to be tracked from discovery through repair.

Manual or Automated

You will find in all books on software testing that automated testing is far better than manual testing. Given the stated benefits of automated testing, why would anyone want to consider manual testing as an option? Well, there are actually certain factors to consider before you decide to automate the testing of your application.

Cost: Manually testing does not require any tools but automated testing requires the purchase of an automated testing tool and training of staff to use the tool.

Software Environment: The environment in which the application was developed is also a factor. Is there a suitable automated testing tool for the environment? And if there is none how feasible is it to build a test harness to test the application?

Testing Type: Testing for such things as ease-of-use of an application cannot be done using an automated testing tool and is best done manually, preferably by usability experts.

TESTING BACK END SYSTEMS

Automated testing tools are most suited for testing front-end systems that users can interact with. This way, interaction with the application can be captured and replayed. However, many applications are built in several tiers with the user interacting with the front end and the back-end existing on a server. These back-end systems can also be tested using an automated approach, but to do this a test harness will need to be built.

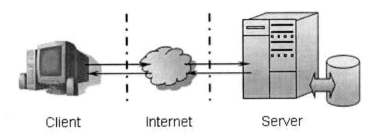

Client   Internet   Server

Figure 2.1:Architecture of a multi-tier application.

The test harness is simply a GUI application that interacts with the back-end system and exercises all relevant portions of the back end system. Figure 2.1 shows the architecture of a multi-tier application indication the front-end test harness and the back-end that is exercised by the test harness. This method has been used to do functional testing on mainframe systems or other back end systems that are not directly supported by your test automation tool.

Manual Testing Process

The manual testing process describes the steps involved in manually testing a software application. This process can be digested into four steps:

1. Plan Test: Plan the tests that will be written by converting the software requirements for the application into test cases. This process was described in the previous chapter.

13

2. Perform Test: Perform each test represented by a test case by performing the user actions. It is important to repeat each step sequentially as directed by the test case

3. Verify Result: Each step with an expected result should be marked as either passed or failed. The existence of a single failed step marks the entire test as failed.

4. Track Defects: For each test that is failed, a defect should be created. This defect should remain open until developers fix the defect and the test is rerun to verify this.

TIP: Even when doing manual testing it is useful to use a test management tool such as Quality Center to manage your test scripts, co-ordinate manual test.

Automated Testing Process

As I have indicated, not all software applications are suited for the automated testing process. However, for those applications that can be tested using the automated approach, the best results can be achieved by using the following steps:

1. Plan Test: This is the same test planning process done in the manual approach to testing. The end result of this approach is the creation of test cases. Please review an example of this in Listing 1.1

2. Create Automated Test: This involves automating the steps described in the test case. Using the facility provided in the automation tool being used. For most test automation tools, this process usually involves

   a. Recording actions performed by the tester and converting this into a macro scripting language

   b. Enhancing the test script to include programmatic verification steps and inclusion of additionally useful code script

3. Debug Test: As with every program, test the functionality of the created test script to ensure that it meets with the original intent. A test that is not fully debugged could generate false positive by highlighting correct application functionality as being defective.

4. Run Test: Once the test is verified, run the test directly or through the use of a scheduling tool.

5. Verify Results: Unlike the manual testing process where results are verified during the execution of the test, the automated testing approach generates comprehensive test results that are stored and can be viewed later to determine the existence of defects. It is important to remember that a major benefit of automated testing is unattended execution of tests so all necessary information should be directed to the test result for later viewing by testers.

6. Track Defects: For failed tests, a defect should be created and tracked through development and subsequent retests.

ASK THE EXPERTS

Q: Is 100% code coverage possible during testing?

A: 100% code coverage, also known as complete application testing is always the goal of testing. This involves completely testing all possible scenarios of the application in order to exercise every line of code. This goal is very difficult to achieve especially for an application of significant size and complexity. That is because as a system grows the direct paths to each feature grows exponentially thereby growing the number of test cases equivalently. Because testing is time constrained, the most frequently used scenarios are often selected for testing.

Mercury Suite of Testing Tools

Mercury Interactive has been at the forefront of software testing with a suite of tools that function together to allow for the testing of software applications on many platforms. They provide tools for all phases of the software testing process including tools for functional testing (WinRunner, QuickTest Professional), performance testing (LoadRunner) and test process management (Quality Center).

WinRunner is a leading part of Mercury's arsenal of tools and it provides testers with the ability to test both Windows and web based application created in several different languages, running on multiple platforms and embedding a variety of technologies. One of the major features of WinRunner is its ease of use, which greatly simplifies the process of test automation and makes it a highly accessible test automation tool. Another very useful feature WinRunner provides is that it integrates easily with other Mercury tools such as:

- Quality Center to provide testers with the ability to create and manage test scripts easily within a single source repository as well as execute these script on any available machine connected to Quality Center.

15

- Loadrunner to allow reuse of scripts that can be used to performance testing and software configuration tuning on *n-tiered* systems.

- QuickTest Professional (QTP) to utilize scripts or functions that might have been created using QTP without the need for replicating the test script in WinRunner. QTP is also an automated testing tool that provides support for some environments not supported by WinRunner.

In this book, I will be concentrating primarily on WinRunner. In the next chapters, I will introduce the WinRunner tool to you and try to help you understand how this powerful tool can be used to easily automate the testing process.

Figure 2.2: Splashscreen of the WinRunner application.

Summary

In this chapter you have learned:

- That the two forms of software testing are manual and automated.

- Benefits of using automated testing approach to test your application.

- When to choose the automated testing approach as opposed to the manual approach.

- The process of testing software applications using the manual approach and the automated approach

- Software provided in the Mercury Suite of testing tools.

CHAPTER 3

IMPORTANT CONCEPTS IN TEST AUTOMATION

In the previous chapters, I have described the process of software development and test automation providing a useful overview of these concepts. Before we begin using WinRunner, I am going to introduce you to additional concepts that relate to test automation. Many of these important concepts are implemented by WinRunner and they form the foundation of how the tool performs certain tasks such as recognizing objects within our applications, recording the actions that we perform and playing back these actions etc.

It is important to note that many of the concepts that I talk about in this chapter are not unique to WinRunner alone but are shared by many testing tools such as Mercury Interactive's QuickTest Professional Compuware's TestPartner etc. In our discussion however, I will concentrate mostly on how WinRunner uses these concepts to allow us create test scripts.

Types of Software Applications

The reason you are reading this book is because you are interested in the process of testing software applications. But what are the different types of software applications? Can you test all these different types of applications in WinRunner? And if not, why not? These are very useful questions to ask and they will all be answered in this section.

There are several different forms of application software that exists with each type tailored for a specific device or platform. Generally called programs these software applications are created for use on the various types of computer systems that exist today such as PDAs, desktops, mainframes etc. These programs are also built using a variety of programming languages and technologies. You may have heard of such languages as C++, Visual Basic, Java etc. These are some of the programming languages that are used to create software applications.

Many of the programs created are specific to an operating system environment that they were designed for. An example of this is Internet Explorer, a desktop application for browsing web sites, will run on the Windows operating system (OS) but will not run on a Mac or Linux OS. Internet Explorer will not even run on all versions of the Windows OS.

Later in this chapter I will describe some of the languages and technologies used in creating these applications. In Table 3.1, I have provided a brief list of the different types of software applications in common use today.

Type	Description
Desktop	Applications that are created to be installed and executed within a PC operating system environment. Desktop applications are the most common form of application software and were historically purchased as shrink-wrapped software. More recently, purchase through Internet downloads has steadily grown.
Web	Applications that are created to be interacted with over a network. Mostly, these applications are accessed over the Internet through the use of a web browser but web applications can also be deployed for use over an intranet.
Embedded	Applications embedded into a specific electronic device. These applications are specific to the device type for which the application is created. Examples of embedded applications include the on-screen menu of your television.
Mobile	Applications designed for small memory footprint devices such as cell phones and PDAs Mobile devices are increasingly being used to perform computing tasks.
Mainframe	Mainframe applications are often highly complex and computation intensive applications that drive the business of an enterprise. Mainframe applications are often accessed using terminal emulation software.

Table 3.1: Types of Application software.

No single software can be created to test all the different types of applications listed here. There are simply too many variations in the technologies and operating systems involved. Of the types of applications listed here, only desktop applications and web applications can be directly tested using WinRunner although there are strategies that can be employed to test mainframe applications or backend systems using WinRunner. I have explored one of those strategies in a sidebar in Chapter 2 titled **Testing Backend Systems**. The complete discussion of these advanced strategies is outside the scope of this book.

Desktop Applications

When the programming code for desktop applications are written, they have to rely on a user interface library to draw the objects used in these applications on the users screen. For instance, objects such as buttons, text boxes, combo boxes etc. are not re-created by every programmer that is writing an application. If this were so, each button in an application would look, feel, and react differently from each other. The objects in a program are reused from an object library that the specific programming language being written depends on.

The Visual C++ programming language for instance would have a different object library than Java, or Visual Basic. Java applications for instance have the ability to add images as contents of a table, but an application written in Visual Basic does not support such a feature. A screenshot of a java application with images included in the Table object is shown in Figure 3.1.

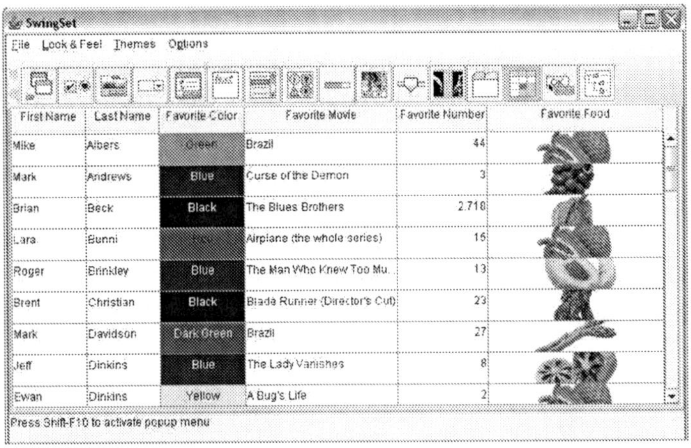

Figure 3.1: Java application with a table containing images.

For a computer to properly run this application the system needs to have the correct object library installed. Without this, the system wouldn't know how to correctly display the intended table object on screen.

Without these object libraries installed on a machine, the application will generate an error whenever it needs any of these objects. You may have seen the image shown in Figure 3.2 before, this is an error users get when they try to run an application created using Visual Basic 6 on their computer without having the proper user interface library installed.

19

Figure 3.2: Error message when the Visual Basic 6 object library is not installed.

In many cases, the application may simply fail to start. The required object libraries are often in the form of files with the following extensions:

- .dll – By far the most common for Windows applications.

- .lib – More common on UNIX systems, although they do the same things as Windows DLLs.

- .ocx – An ActiveX object, also known as a COM object.

- .jar – Used for Java applications.

Web Applications

WinRunner can test web applications regardless of the programming language used to create the web application. This is because when testing web applications, we are not interacting natively with the web application. Instead, we issue requests to the web server that the web application is running on using the HTTP protocol and the web server processes our request and responds in HTML format. The response is then displayed within our web browser.

To verify that a web application works correctly we simply need to verify that for a given input (this is called a request), the application provides an appropriate output (known as a response). Figure 3.3 shows this Request/Response model that is used in web applications.

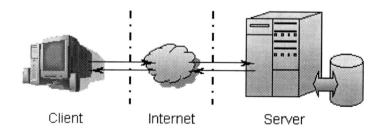

Client   Internet   Server

Figure 3.3: Request/Response model of web applications.

Some of the common languages in use for creating web applications include ASP.NET, Java/J2EE, PHP, Cold Fusion, Perl etc. This list is by no means exhaustive because any programming language that exists can be used in creating a web application as long as the language implements either the Common Gateway Interface (CGI) protocol or can process HTTP requests. Because we only interact with a web application using HTTP and HTML, these source languages are not important to us and we do not need to have any object library for the programming language installed on our machine. The objects within HTML are the only objects that we need, and our browsers already know how to display those. All that we need to have is a web browser. These days, virtually all operating systems come bundled with a least one web browser. The result of this process to us is that WinRunner can test web applications written in any source language as long as you load the web add-in.

Sometimes, web applications can also embed a variety of objects within their page. These embedded technologies are known as plug-in technologies and they often provide useful functionality to the web page that uses them. Some of the most common plug-in technologies are listed in Table 3.2.

Plug-in	Description
ActiveX	Created using a variety of languages such as VB, C++ or Delphi
Applets	Created using Java language.
Flash	Created using the ActionScript language

Table 3.2: Plug-ins found in web applications.

Each of plug-ins types mentioned in Table 3.2 above, have the ability to provide application-like functionality to a web application. When these plug-ins are used the web page is said to have rich web functionality.

Several companies make use of these plug-ins because of the expanded function they provide to a web page. Also, some companies may not want users to download their applications but instead have users interact with the application as a plug-in while using their browser.

Record/Playback

One of the biggest benefits of automated testing is the ability to perform a series of actions and have the automated testing tool record these actions and then play it back in exactly the same way as the action was initially performed. It is immediately obvious that this saves the tester a lot of time. To support the recording of actions, the automated testing tool must overcome two challenges:

1. Find a way to recognize objects

2. Find a way to represent what actions users perform in code form.

To record what is being done, the system must find a way to recognize the object that the user is performing an operation on. This way, when we playback the actions the system can perform the operations on the correct objects. If an application has two buttons such as in Figure 3.4 below, the system must record the correct button that the user clicked on because each button performs a different operation. If the testing tool clicks on a different button from the one the tester clicked on, the test would be invalid. The process of identifying objects within an AUT is known as object recognition.

Once the automated tool can identify the object we used in an operation, it must also have a way to record what we did to the object. Did we click on it? Type text into it? Select from it? In short, the system must observe the operation we performed with an object and then represent this operation in a form that allows it to play back the operation correctly. This process is known as representing operations.

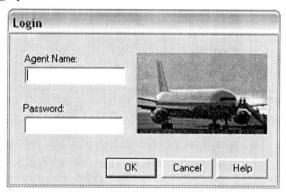

Figure 3.4: The Flight Reservation application.

Object Recognition

The problem of object recognition is a tricky one. Imagine receiving computer help over the phone when the caller tells you what to do to your machine by describing the objects they want you to interact with. For instance, if they want you to open the control panel (on a Windows XP machine), the steps involved might sound like:

1. Click the button on your taskbar that has the word 'Start'
2. Click on the Control Panel list item in the displayed menu

22

In this instance, you are provided with enough description to uniquely identify an object you need to interact with. If you have two buttons, with the word 'Start' on them in your taskbar, then an additional piece of description must be provided such as:

1. Click the leftmost button on your task bar, that has the word 'Start'

This additional piece of information is essential in order to uniquely identify the correct object. This is the same process employed by WinRunner, it simply records a description of each object you interact with in your application into a file. The way it records the description is by noting enough property/value pairs of an object that uniquely describe the object. Additionally, to make it easy to reference the object at a later time, it provides a logical name for the object. The logical name is simply an alias. This way, instead of saying:

1. Click the leftmost button on your task bar, that has the word 'Start'

I can use a logical name such as btnStart and describe the operation as:

1. Click btnStart

This latter form is more succinct and less open to interpretation errors.

There are three tools used by WinRunner for this operation and these include GUI Spy, GUI Configuration and GUI Map Editor. I will discuss these objects at length in later chapters. For now, it is more important to understand the concept that in order to teach automated testing tools how to interact with your application, these tools must record descriptions of the objects you interact with and map these descriptions to a logical name. Expectedly the name of the resulting mapping file will differ from one tool to another.

Representing Operations

Every automated testing tool has a built-in script language that it uses to record operations performed on the AUT by the tester. When a tester performs an operation, the testing tool records the object that the user performs the test on and also the type of operation that was performed. The tool then translates the operation performed into the appropriate syntax of its built-in script language.

If you have used a macro recording tool at some point, you may have some familiarity with this concept. Microsoft Office is perhaps the most used macro tool allowing mini script to be created using the Visual Basic for Applications (VBA) language. For WinRunner, the script language used is Test Script Language (TSL) and for QTP, the language used is VBScript. In TSL, the operation of closing a window is represented in code as:

```
win_close ("frmExpense");
```

While in VBScript this operation is represented as:

```
VBWindow("frmExpense").Close
```

I will not delve into the intricacies of script languages at this point, but you will notice that both languages reference an object name, and the operation to perform on the object. Later in the book, I will introduce you to the TSL language.

ASK THE EXPERTS

Q: What is the difference between a script language and a programming language?

A: A script language can be described as a diluted version of a programming language. Whereby programming languages have the capacity of creating complete application with various uses and functionality, script languages most exist to perform less complex object manipulation, computation and reporting functionalities. For this reason, script languages are much smaller in size and therefore much easier to learn.

Add-In Architecture

Before an application can be tested, it is important for the testing tool to understand the technology used in building the application. This means to test an application that was written in the Visual Basic programming language, WinRunner must understand the objects that exist within a Visual Basic application and the methods/properties of these objects.

At development time, the developers of your automation testing tool cannot know what type of application you intend to test so they have the option of hard-coding the knowledge of how to test Visual Basic applications into your automated testing tool. This will teach the tool how to handle applications written in Visual Basic. But what happens when the version of Visual Basic changes? You would need to update the entire application? And what if you want to test a Java application and not a Visual Basic application? Well, the system would still load the hard-coded Visual Basic knowledge even though you are not using it.

Clearly, this format is very resource inefficient. The more efficient solution would be to choose the modules you want your automated testing tool to load based on the application you are testing. So, for a Java application, you can load the Java module and your automated testing tool immediately knows how to test applications written in Java.

This is known as a pluggable architecture and the benefits of this architecture include:

24

- Reduction in memory footprint - WinRunner does not have to load information for how to interact with all supported environments at the same time. It simply provides a core set of support and allows users to specify the additional add-ins they wish to use.

- Extensibility - WinRunner can continue to create add-ins for new technologies even after their product has been shipped. Users that need the new functionality would simply need to buy and install the add-in and have that available to them.

Figure 3.5: WinRunner Add-In Manager.

Parameterizing Tests

WinRunner provides a tool that can be used to dynamically pass values to test scripts and thus avoid the lure of hard coding information into your test scripts. This way, a single test script can execute using different sets of sample data. For example, in an application involving the creation of expense records, the operation of creating the record will be the same and the content of what is being added may be different each time. Using data parameters we will be able to record this operation once and using dynamic parameters from your data table, run the test multiple times adding a different record to the application each time.

The values from the data table are used to replace the hard-coded values recorded into your test script in a process known as parameterization. Parameterization provides testers with the flexibility of determining what data values their test script will use at run time. Without this, you will need to edit your test script every time to replace your hard-coded values. This would affect the frequency of execution of the test script and also subject your test script to potential errors when users have to edit the script to replace values.

So what is this data table? The data table is simply an Excel spreadsheet that is stored within your test folder. It is editable in WinRunner through the Data Table editor but can also be directly edited in Microsoft Excel or any application capable of open Excel documents such as OpenOffice Calc.

Figure 3.6 shows the Data Table editor in WinRunner.

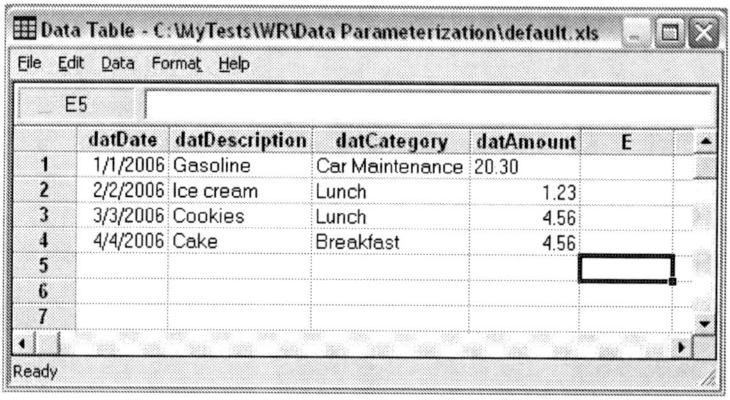

Figure 3.6: WinRunner Data Table editor.

Summary

In this chapter you have learned:

- The different types of software applications that exist.

- Features of desktop as well as web applications.

- The concept of recording a test using an automated tool and playing back the recording

- What an add-in is and how add-in architectures helps create compact and responsive automated testing tools.

- The concept of data parameterization and how it helps make automated tests more dynamic.

CHAPTER 4

INTRODUCING WINRUNNER

Now that you are familiar with the process of test automation in general, I am going to get more specific about the test automation tool that we will be exploring in this book. The automated testing tool we will be working with is WinRunner version 8.0. This software provides automated software testing support for desktop applications created for the Windows platform and also for web applications. If you have a different version of WinRunner, you may still be able to follow along with this book, as there are mostly incremental changes between versions.

At the time of this writing, Mercury Interactive still offers fully functional, limited-time evaluation copies of WinRunner 8. You can download this from the Mercury Interactive website (www.mercuryinteractive.com) and use it and follow along.

Launching WinRunner

WinRunner installs into the program menu like most Windows applications. You will have to navigate to Programs ▶ WinRunner ▶ WinRunner to launch the tool. If you use WinRunner frequently, you should create a shortcut and place it on your desktop so that you can conveniently launch the application.

TIP: Whenever WinRunner is running, an icon for the WinRunner Record/Run engine is shown in the status area of the taskbar. If your WinRunner session crashes, you must close this engine by clicking on the icon and selecting Close WinRunner from the context menu.

If your system does not have WinRunner as an item in the program menu, navigate to C:\Program Files\Mercury Interactive\WinRunner\arch\wrun.exe on your system and then create a shortcut to this executable. If you still can't find this file, then search the entire system for wrun.exe. Don't forget that the installation folder can be changed during installation so you may have to search the entire filesystem. This process should work in the large majority of instances, but if you still cannot run WinRunner on your machine, check with the person that installed the software on your system.

WinRunner Environment

Now that we have invoked the WinRunner application, I will introduce you to the different tools, dialogs and windows that make up WinRunner. As a standard Windows application, WinRunner provides support for such items as menus, toolbars, a status bar and docked windows. You may be already familiar with these components through using other applications, although the actual/toolbar items in WinRunner differ from other products, the concepts are similar. I have provided in Figure 4.1 an example of the WinRunner main window. Before we review the contents of this main window, let us take a stepwise walk through the preliminary dialogs that you will see when you launch WinRunner and what these dialogs are used for.

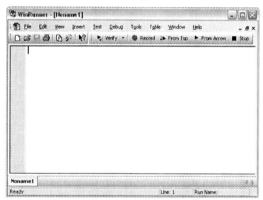

Figure 4.1: The WinRunner Window.

Add-In Manager

On launching WinRunner, the first dialog that you will see is the WinRunner Add-in Manager. WinRunner uses an *add-in architecture* to teach the testing environment how to handle objects created using different technologies. Without loading add-ins, the core WinRunner application is only capable of recognizing objects built upon the standard Windows environment and based upon the Microsoft Foundation Class (MFC) library of objects. If you attempt

28

to interact with an application written using a different technology such as Visual Basic or Java, WinRunner will expectedly not know how to properly identify objects within your application. Until the appropriate add-in is installed and loaded, WinRunner will remain unaware of how to properly recognize the objects within your application.

Figure 4.2: WinRunner Add-In architecture.

Figure 4.2 shows the WinRunner add-in architecture with a list of add-ins installed on a system. You can choose as many of these add-ins as necessary to test your application. This means that to test an application in WinRunner, you must know the appropriate add-ins to use. Table 4.1 below provides a list of some of the available add-ins, and what environment they are used for. The Availability column shows the add-ins that are included in the initial WinRunner installation.

Add-in	Availability	Use
PowerBuilder	Built-in	Used to test any Windows application created using the PowerBuilder programming language.
ActiveX Controls	Built-in	Used to test ActiveX components. ActiveX technology was described in Chapter 3.
Delphi	Licensed	Used to test applications written in the Delphi language. Delphi is the object-oriented Version of the Pascal programming language.
ERP	Licensed	Add-ins supporting several Enterprise Resource Planning systems including Baan, Oracle Applications, Peoplesoft, SAP, Siebel. These add-ins need to be individually purchased.
Java	Licensed	Used to test applications and applets created using Sun Microsystem's Java programming language.
Visual Basic	Built-in	Used to test applications created in the Visual Basic language. This does not include

		applications created with VB.NET
WAP	Licensed	Used to test applications that support the Wireless Application Protocol standard.
WebTest	Built-in	Used to test any type of HTML based web application that you interact with using a web browser.[#]

Table 4.1: Some WinRunner add-ins and their uses.

[#] The language used in creating a web application is not important for the automated testing of *web* applications. Therefore WinRunner can easily test web applications created in any programming language.

The information about the add-in you intend to load must be furnished to WinRunner through the Add-In Manager. Figure 4.3 shows this Add-In manager and the check boxes that you must select to choose a specific add-in. This is the first screen that loads in WinRunner because it informs the tool about the add-ins you want to use during your testing session.

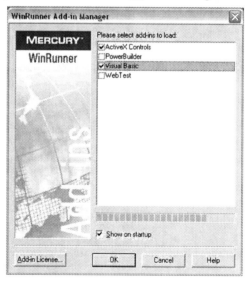

Figure 4.3: The Add-In manager.

In Figure 4.3, I have chosen the ActiveX Controls and Visual Basic add-ins.

NOTE: The Add-In Manager can be disabled from showing up at start-up in the General Options dialog. It can also be re-enabled from the same dialog.

Welcome Screen

On startup of the application, the user is greeted by the Welcome screen. The Welcome screen provides users with a few helpful choices on what to do with their current session. As shown in Figure 4.4, the choices provided include:

- Create a New Test – Choose this option if you wish to start working on a new, empty, test.

- Open an Existing test – Choose this option if you wish to continue working on a previously created test.

- View a Quick Preview of WinRunner – Choose this option to launch a browser-based preview of the WinRunner tool. New users can use this handy guide to learn some of WinRunner's features.

- Exit – Choose this option to close the Welcome screen.

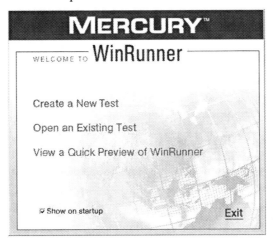

Figure 4.4: The Welcome Screen.

After a while, you will find the welcome screen rather unnecessary. You can easily disable it by un-checking the *Show on startup* checkbox on the Welcome dialog.

NOTE: The Welcome screen can be disabled/enabled to display at start-up by changing the WinRunner General Options dialog.

WinRunner Application

The next window that we will discuss is the WinRunner main application window. This is the main window of the automated testing tool and is the part of the application you will primarily use during your test creation and execution. As with most GUI applications, there are sections of this tool that you will be immediately familiar with.

The WinRunner main application window is a typical Windows Multiple Document Interface (MDI) application consisting of menus, toolbars, a status bar and dockable document windows. Unlike some other editors, WinRunner has the capacity to edit multiple test files at the same time. Each document window contains a test file that is accessible via a tab corresponding to the test name. You can switch easily between the tests being created by clicking the tab for the test you want to view. You can also switch between tests by clicking the Window menu and selecting the test you want to work with. Figure 4.5 shows WinRunner with several tests open. Notice the location of the tabs for choosing the test you want to edit.

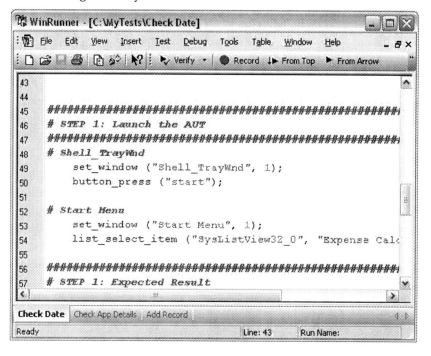

Figure 4.5: WinRunner with multiple open documents.

The menus in WinRunner provide access to multiple tools and functionality that can be used for various tasks such as editing, debugging, and file management; the toolbars provide a quick access mechanism to useful menuitems and the document dialogs allows you to view/modify files of various types.

Table 4.2 lists the menus available within WinRunner as well as the functions provided by the menuitems within these menus.

Menu	Function
File	Contains file management functions such as opening, saving and printing files. Also provides access to setting properties for the test and opening recent tests.
Edit	Provides editing functionality to a test such as undo, redo, cut, copy, paste, delete etc.
View	Allows you to toggle the toolbars and status bar and also customize the toolbar contents.
Insert	Contains tools for the inclusion of several forms of test artifacts including checkpoints, synchronization points and TSL functions.
Test	Contains tools for controlling recording, playback and choosing execution mode.
Debug	Contains tools for debugging a test including breakpoints, stepping tools and adding data watches.
Tools	Allows you to configure options in WinRunner and also contains many tools for managing GUI Maps, connecting to Quality Center, launching the Test Result tool, create Recovery Scenarios etc.
Table	Tools for dealing with the WinRunner data table and parameterizing tests.
Window	Provides the ability to manage the multiple test windows open in WinRunner.
Help	Contains access to WinRunner help files, tutorials and user guides. Also contains licensing information about your WinRunner installation as well as links to the Mercury website.

Table 4.2: List of WinRunner menus.

As is typical with many GUI applications, WinRunner has several toolbars. Each toolbar provide a convenient way to access those menu functions that are used more often. Figure 4.6 shows the toolbars that are available within WinRunner. A description of each of these toolbars is shown in Table 4.3 below.

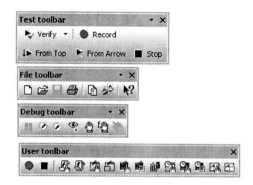

Figure 4.6: The WinRunner toolbars.

Menu	Function
File	Contains file management functions.
Test	Contains tools for controlling recording, playback and choosing execution mode.
Debug	Contains tools for debugging a test including breakpoints, stepping tools and adding data watches.
User	Contains a combination of tools that can be used for test creation, debugging, and execution.

Table 4.3: List of WinRunner toolbars.

WinRunner also provides the ability to customize the included toolbars. This way, you may choose to add the commands that you use more frequently and remove others.

TIP: WinRunner's toolbars can be displayed as dockable or floating items allowing you to move the toolbars around to a location.

There are also several wizards available within WinRunner. I will be describing of these as we come across them in later chapters.

TIP: The status bar in WinRunner provides several useful pieces of information such as the current command, line number of the cursor, and test run name. The status bar can be enabled/disabled by clicking View ▶ Status Bar.

Debug Viewer

On completion of a test, it is important to exercise the test a few times to ensure that the test functions exactly as intended. Because test scripts contain programmable logic just like the applications we are testing, it is rather easy to see that our tests can also contain defects. The major difference between possible defects in our test script and defects in the AUT is that our test script contains far fewer lines of code than the AUT. This makes it much easier to discover any defects that exist within the test.

The process of debugging can be described as slowing down execution of test script to the line based level and using tools to inspect the elements within the test script. Do our variables contain the expected value? When did the value change? What does a specific function call do? The debugging process aids us in answering these questions and by doing so we can figure out any error that may exist in our test script.

The Debug Viewer shown in Figure 4.7 is one of the tools provided by WinRunner to aid in application debugging. It is a collection of 3 tools, with each tool displayed in a separate tab of the Debug Viewer.

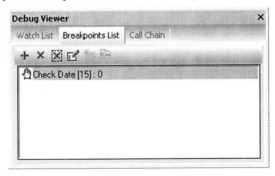

Figure 4.7: The Debug Viewer.

Watch List – Provides the ability to define expressions and inspect the value of these expressions. Variables are expressions and can therefore be added to the watch list.

Breakpoint List – Shows a list of breakpoints within the test including line-based and function based breakpoints.

Call Chain – Provides a stepwise list of calls made in a test including any functions invoked in the call stack.

35

Function Viewer

During test execution, several functions are loaded into memory whenever they are invoked. The Function Viewer provides the ability to view all the functions loaded into WinRunner's memory space. This tool also provides the ability to load functions from within a compiled module. Figure 4.8 shows the function Viewer.

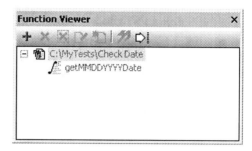

Figure 4.8: The Function Viewer.

The Function Viewer exists in a dockable window and can be launched using the menu by clicking Tools ▶ Function Viewer.

Exiting WinRunner

To conclude a WinRunner session, click on File ▶ Exit from the WinRunner menu. If you have any unsaved tests, WinRunner will prompt you to save them. You may choose not to do so. You may also exit WinRunner by clicking on the terminate button of the Window.

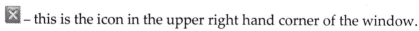 – this is the icon in the upper right hand corner of the window.

Once WinRunner is no longer running, the WinRunner icon will no longer be visible in the status area of the Windows Taskbar.

Summary

In this chapter you have learned:

- How to invoke and exit WinRunner.

- The different windows that are available in WinRunner and their usage in testing applications.

- The different menus and toolbars that exist within WinRunner and the functionality that these items provide.

CHAPTER 5

USING WINRUNNER

In chapter 2, I described the process of testing using automated testing tools. That description was provided in broad terms to cover most automated testing tools. We will now look closely at the process of test automation using WinRunner. That is, of course, the primary reason you are reading this book.

WinRunner Testing Roadmap

The WinRunner test automation process can best be described as a series of five individual steps. Each step has to be performed in sequence because every later step has a dependency on the prior step. You must for instance, create a GUI Map before you can create a test. I have provided below each of these steps and a lengthy description of what each step entails:

1. Teach WinRunner to recognize objects in your application.

In order to successfully repeat the operations that you perform on an application, WinRunner must learn to recognize the objects within your application. This process is known as object identification and it involves creating a mapping file that associates the GUI objects within your AUT to a set of logical names. The logical names would be used within your test whenever you interact with objects in the application.

The object identification process creates an object-mapping file known as a GUI Map file. The main tool used in creating this file is known as the GUI Map Editor. The GUI Map file contains a list of property/value pairs for each object within your AUT. The properties that are recorded by the GUI Map Editor and used to identify the object are controlled by the GUI Configuration tool.

Figure 5.1: The GUI Map Configuration tool.

CAUTION: Though the GUI Map file is an ASCII file, it should never be directly edited. All editing should be done through the GUI Map editor.

Creating the GUI Map file needs to be done only once for an application being tested. All the tests that are created will then make use of this GUI Map file.

2. Create Test

The test creation process creates the actual test script that will test your application's functionality. The result of this process is a script file that contains Test Script Language (TSL) code as well as several test artifacts stored in your test folder. The test creation process can be broken down into two steps.

a. *Record test*
    This involves performing a series of actions that are a part of a business process. WinRunner will record these actions by creating corresponding TSL statements (to match the operations being performed) into your test script.

b. *Enhance test*
    The recorded test contains the operations performed by the user but it does not perform any verification. A test must have at least one verification included (shown in the expected results column I mentioned in Chapter 1). Without verification, how would you know that the AUT correctly performed the intended operation? However, since verification

steps and some other useful features cannot be recorded, they have to be manually inserted into the test.

These are enhancements to your test and the various types of enhancements that can be edited into your test are:

i. Synchronization point – Used to pause execution of the WinRunner test for a specific amount of time, or until a specific event occurs. This is a useful feature for handling timing issues such as cases where an operation might take an indefinite amount of time to complete.

    E.g. when you log into an application, the time duration for logging in may vary greatly based on the number of users working on the application.

ii. Checkpoint – Checks to ensure that when an application reaches a specific step in its execution, it has a certain predetermined value. WinRunner provides four checkpoints that can easily be used to verify application functionality.

    E.g. when you exit an application by clicking File ▶ Exit, you expect the window to close.

iii. Data parameterization – The ability to remove hard-coded values from within a test and replace these with values read from a stored spreadsheet. This allows us to run the same test several times using a different set of input values for each test run.

iv. Scripting – Addition of TSL code to the test. For expert programmers, adding TSL can make a test significantly robust. It can eliminate most instances where manual intervention is required and also make the test less error-prone. Also, there are certain functionality that can only be checked using TSL code.

    E.g. verifying that the application displays the correct system date.

3. Debugging the Test

Running the test a few times after creation is important to ensure that the test works appropriately. The goal of debugging is to identify any errors that exist within your test and then fix these problems. Errors in test scripts include TSL syntax problems, or semantic errors. Any of these errors in a test makes the test operate incorrectly and clearly invalidates the test results. Would you want to rely on the results of a bad test?

While debugging a test in WinRunner, we run the test in a mode known as Debug Run mode. This tells WinRunner to overwrite the results of the test every time we run the test thereby saving disk space. WinRunner also provides a comprehensive set of tools that are useful for pausing test execution, executing TSL code one line at a time and examining the contents of memory during execution. These tools work together to make it easy to find problems in a test and fix those problems.

4. Running the tests

Once your debugging process has given the test a clean bill of health, you can now start running the test in a mode known as Verify Run mode. In this mode, all test results are assigned a unique run name and the results are preserved in a different folder on your file-system. Note that this differs from Debug Run mode where previous test results are overwritten.

Execution of tests can be done in a variety of ways such as executing the test directly through WinRunner, or using a test management tool such as TestDirector to schedule execution.

5. Analyze the test results

WinRunner provides a Test Result viewer that can be used to view the results of a test execution. This tool allows us to view several important details about the test execution such as execution date, time, and overall results etc. Additionally, if a checkpoint step fails, we can get detailed information about why the failure happened such as the actual value found within the application during the execution.

These five steps are important to every tester using WinRunner as they represent the lifecycle process that will be repeated several times during the testing of a project.

Introduction to Expense Calculator

In this book, I'll be using a small Windows based application to illustrate the testing concepts that are being discussed. The application is named Expense Calculator and it is an application designed for managing daily expenses.

Expense Calculator was designed to be compact and simple in order to allow me to illustrate many of the testing concepts without including a large amount of unnecessary TSL code. Figure 5.2 shows the main window of the application.

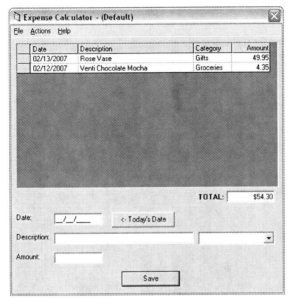

Figure 5.2: Main window of Expense Calculator.

In this book, Expense Calculator is the *Application Under Test* (AUT). The application makes use of the following technologies:

Visual Basic 6.0 – The programming language used to create the application.

COM (ActiveX Controls) – The MSFlexGrid and MaskedEdit controls are used to display and validate data respectively.

OLE Database – An ADO datasource, specifically a Microsoft Access database, is used by the application for data storage. The database is located in the same folder where the executable application is installed and named expcalc.mdb.

NOTE: You can download the entire Expense Calculator project including requirements & design documents, code and installation files at http://genixpress.com/gp/files/WISS.zip.

Installing Expense Calculator

The following process should be used in installing the Expense Calculator application.

1. Use your browser to download the zip file for Expense Calculator from http://www.genixpress.com/gp/files/WISS.zip to any folder on your computer. This file contains the requirements documents, design documents, source code and installer for expense calculator.

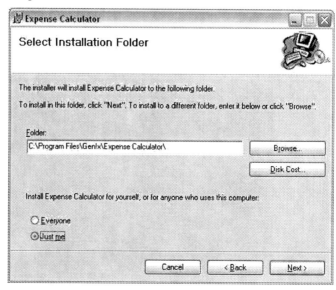

Figure 5.3: Expense Calculator installation program page.

2. Using a zip extraction tool such as Winzip (www.winzip.com), extract the content into a folder on your computer.

3. Using Windows Explorer, locate the folder you extracted the files into. Open the Deployment folder and within this, you will find a file named Expense Calculator.msi. This is the installer.

4. Run this installer, by double-clicking the file. Figure 5.3 shows the main installer page. I suggest that you accept the default settings, but if you are comfortable with application installation, you may modify the settings to suit your preferences.

CAUTION: If you change the installation location, you must remember the folder you specify and make similar adjustments whenever I refer to the installation folder later in the book.

Once you have installed Expense Calculator, you will be able to follow along with the test cases that are being created in this book.

Summary

In this chapter you have learned:

- The process to follow when doing testing using WinRunner.
- Details about the application that we will be testing in this book.
- How to install the Expense Calculator application.

CHAPTER 6

MAPPING THE GUI

As you have learned in Chapter 5, the first step in creating a test involves the creation of an object-mapping file. Windows applications are often made up of a collection of GUI (Graphical User Interface) objects. These objects, such as buttons, check boxes, lists etc make up the look and feel of the application. Additionally, each of the objects has a list of physical properties such as height, width, label etc. For WinRunner to appropriately identify objects within our AUT, it needs to have a description of each of the object created and saved to a file. This file is an object-mapping file and is called the GUI Map file.

The concept here is similar to what is involved when someone is helping you on phone with a problem on your computer. They may say something like:

Click on the button in the Windows taskbar that has the label Start. From the list that is displayed click on an item titled My Documents. A window will pop up with My Document as the caption. In this window, click on a menuitem with the caption of Help, and within this menu list that drops down, click on the menuitem captioned About Windows...

What is being done here is that the properties of each object on the screen are being used to specify the object you should interact with. The object-mapping file that WinRunner creates, i.e. the GUI Map file, does the same thing. It stores the description of objects within a single file and then assigns to each of these objects an alias known as logical name. For the statement above, imagine if we began by creating a simple mapping file as shown in Table 6.1 below:

Alias	Description
btnStart	The Start button in the Windows taskbar.
lstMyDocuments	The list item title My Documents displayed in the programs list

	of the Windows system.
wndMyDocuments	The windows displayed when the My Documents icon is clicked on.
mnuHelp	The menuitem titled Help in the My Documents window.
mnuAbout	The sub menu of the Help menu, titled About.

Table 6.1: A simple mapping file.

This allows us to now repeat the description in a more simplified form as:

Click on btnStart. From the displayed list click on lstMyDocuments. wndMyDocuments will pop up. In this window, click on mnuHelp and then click on mnuAbout...

The description is greatly simplified because we are using the aliases we created previously and so the objects are easily identifiable. The benefit here is greatly amplified when you need to perform multiple operations on these objects and instead of having to describe them over and over, you can simply refer to their alias. This is what WinRunner does. Listing 6.1 shows a small snippet from the GUI Map file that is created in WinRunner.

```
frmAbout:
{
 class: window,
 label: "About Expense Calculator",
 MSW_class: ThunderRT6FormDC
}
frmAbout.btnOK:
{
 class: push_button,
 MSW_id: 1
}
frmAbout.btnSystemInfo:
{
 class: push_button,
 vb_name: cmdSysInfo
}
frmExpense.btnDate:
{
 class: push_button,
 vb_name: btnToday
}
frmExpense.btnSave:
{
 class: push_button,
 vb_name: btnSave
```

}

Listing 6.1: Partial contents of a GUI Map file.

Listing 6.1 shows that similar to our example, WinRunner uses the properties of objects to describe them and then assigns them a logical name. This logical name would be what we use in our script. The object map should contains all objects within the AUT and a logical name is assigned to this object, this way, in our tests, we refer to the logical names and WinRunner interacts with the appropriate object.

OBJECT ORIENTED PROGRAMMING

With the growth of systems with a graphical interface, it became necessary to view components within an application from a perspective that would make it easier to write applications for a multi-tasking windowed system. The Object Oriented Programming paradigm emerged as a way to view items within an application as virtual objects with the following intrinsic features:

Properties – attributes possessed by an object.

Methods – Built-in functionality of objects.

Events – operations that can be performed on an object.

Object Oriented Programming (or OOP as it is more commonly known) additionally describes certain features and functionalities that objects possess, these are however out of the scope of this book. For creating our GUI Map, we use the properties of these objects to describe the objects.

GUI Map File Modes

WinRunner supports 2 modes for dealing with the GUI Map file. These modes are:

GUI Map per test mode

In this mode, a GUI Map file is automatically created for each test you create and WinRunner manages the GUI Map file. This step is appealing because it reduces the initial overhead of creating the GUI Map file. However, if an object in your AUT changes, you are faced with the daunting task of modifying several GUI Map files.

Global GUI Map file mode

In this mode, a GUI Map file is created for an application and all the tests written for that application reference the same GUI Map file. The efficiency of this approach is that if an object changes in your AUT, you can modify the description of the object in this single GUI Map file and all your tests will immediately pick up the changes.

You can specify the mode you want to use in the WinRunner options by navigating to Tools ▶ General Options ▶ General ▶ GUI map file mode. By default, WinRunner is set up to use the Global GUI Map File mode and this is recommended for most of the testing you will do in WinRunner. For an ad-hoc testing session (see Glossary for definition) you may want to use the GUI Map File per Test mode.

In this book, we will be using the Global GUI Map File mode, and all our subsequent tests will reference this file. Next I will describe the tools used in creating a GUI Map file and show you how to create one.

GUI Map File Tools

The GUI Map creation process is a simple one. There are four tools that exist within WinRunner for this operation. Each of the tools provides a small part of the required functionality of creating and managing a GUI Map file. In Table 6.2, I have described the tools involved in this process.

NOTE: Creating the GUI Map file is the first step in our testing process.

Tools	Description
GUI Map Configuration	Allows you to specify the properties for objects that will be recorded.
GUI Spy	Shows all the properties of an object including properties that would be recorded into a GUI map.
GUI Map Editor	Used to create a new GUI Map file or edit an existing one.
GUI Map File Merge	Used to merge the contents of multiple GUI map files into a single file.

Table 6.2: Tools for working with GUI Map files.

All these tools are available within the Tools top level menu in WinRunner. Now that you have been introduced to these tools, we will now look closely at how to use each one of them

GUI Map Configuration

The first challenge in creating a GUI Map is to identify the correct properties to record. If we record too many properties, then if the object changes WinRunner will no longer recognize the object. If we record too few, then WinRunner may not be able to *uniquely* identify the appropriate object.

The goal is therefore to record just enough properties to uniquely identify all the AUT's objects. To a novice this would be a daunting task, but WinRunner has made it relatively pain free. For starters, they have provided the GUI Map Configuration tool which can be used to specify the properties we wish to record for each type of object.

NOTE: The GUI Map Configuration tool can be launched by clicking Tools ▶ GUI Map Configuration.

Better yet, this tool has been pre-configured and can be used properly right out of the box. This means that without any adjustments, you can begin recording and WinRunner will use the default settings of the GUI Map Configuration tool to determine what properties to record for your object. I strongly advise that as new user, you should use these default values. As you get more comfortable with the WinRunner environment however, you may be interested in specifying the properties you want to record for each object.

CAUTION: Changes to the GUI Map Configuration affect every test that is subsequently recorded on the machine. If you want to reverse your changes, hit the default button.

GUI Spy

The GUI Spy is a useful tool for viewing all the properties of an object as well as the values of each property. As I have already indicated earlier, all objects in the AUT have properties and each property of an object has a value. An object such as a button may have properties such as height, width, caption etc. The corresponding values of this properties may be 25, 97 and Save.

The tool shows you the properties of your object that have been/or will be recorded into a GUI Map file. The GUI Spy is additionally very useful when creating checkpoints. it allows us to know the correct values to check for. We discuss the use of this tool for checkpoint creation in Chapter 10.

In the following Quicksteps section, I have provided with details on how to use the GUI Spy.

1. Launch the GUI Spy by clicking on Tools ▶ GUI Spy.

2. Choose whether you want to view properties of an object or of a window.

3. Click on the Spy button with the pointer icon.

4. Move your cursor over the object your want to view.

5. Press Ctrl_L + F3 (i.e. the left Control key and the F3 button together).

On completion of step 5, the information about the object is frozen into the GUI Spy tool. As shown in Figure 6.1, the GUI Spy has three main tabs:

Recorded - Shows the property/value pairs of the object that will be recorded into the GUI Map file based on the configuration information in the GUI Map Configuration tool.

All Standard - Shows the property/value pairs for all the standard properties of the object.

ActiveX - Shows the list of ActiveX properties belonging to an object together with the values. This tab is only available when the Visual Basic or ActiveX Controls add-in is installed.

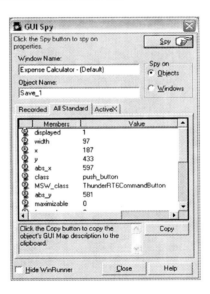

Figure 6.1: The GUI Spy tool.

GUI Map Editor

This is the main tool for use in creating the GUI Map file. While the GUI Map configuration chooses the properties of the object to record, and the GUI Spy displays the properties and their value, the GUI Map Editor actually creates the GUI Map file. This editor allows you to either create a new GUI Map file or edit an existing one. Even with these features, it is a rather simple tool to use. You simply launch the editor, open the relevant GUI Map file and choose the objects you want to record.

Next, we will go through the process of learning all the objects within our AUT.

1. Launch the GUI Map Editor.

This can be done by clicking Tools ▶ GUI Map Editor from the menu. Figure 6.2 shows the tool once launched.

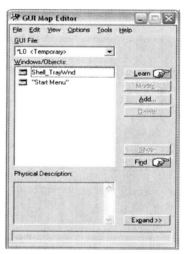

Figure 6.2: The GUI Map Editor.

2. Close all open GUI Map files.

Because we are recording a new GUI Map file, click on File ▶ Close All in the editor's menu. This closes any open GUI Map file. If you want to edit an existing GUI Map file by adding objects or removing objects, you will want to click on File ▶ Open from the editor menu and choose the correct GUI Map file from the filesystem. I will not do this because we are creating a new file.

3. Launch your AUT.

It is important for your application to be displayed on screen if you want to record the objects of the application.

4. Learn the object.

Click on the learn button in the editor and your cursor becomes a pointer. You must then click on the object you intend to learn. It is very important that you do not click on an intermediate object such as the Windows taskbar. When you click on an object that is a window, WinRunner gives you the option of learning all the objects in that window. Figure 6.3 shows you the dialog that is provided when the Expense Calculator main window is clicked on. Clicking the No button adds only the window object, but clicking Yes adds all the objects in the window.

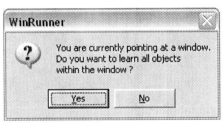

Figure 6.3: Confirmation dialog for the GUI Map Editor.

You will need to repeat this step until all the objects in the AUT have been recorded into the GUI Map file.

5. Save the GUI Map file.

Click on File ▶ Save in the editor menu. This provides a save file dialog that requires you to specify a GUI Map file name. For out AUT, I have saved the GUI Map file as ExpenseCalculator.gui and stored this in the C:\MyTests folder. It is helpful to have the GUI Map file name match the application but this is not a necessity.

NOTE: The GUI Map file that we created can only be used in Global GUI Map file mode.

GUI Map File Merge Tool

If you have recorded the objects in your application into several small GUI Map files, you may later want to combine these objects into a single file. The GUI Map editor can be used to combine the contents of several GUI Map files into one, but this process is entirely manual. To speed up this aggregation activity, WinRunner provides the GUI Map File Merge Tool.

Shown in Figure 6.4, the GUI Map Merge tool allows you to combine the objects within one or more GUI Map files into another GUI Map file. To simplify this process of merging the supports the ability to automate the combination of files. Using the GUI Map Merge Tool is quite easy, we have provided the steps in the QuickSteps section below.

Figure 6.4: The GUI Map Merge Tool.

QUICKSTEPS: USING THE GUI MAP FILE MERGE TOOL

1.   Launch the GUI Map File Merge Tool by clicking on Tools ▶ Merge GUI Map File.

2.   Choose whether you want to do a Manual Merge or an Auto Merge.

3.   Specify a target file you wish to merge the GUI Map files into.

4.   Enter one or more source files that you want to merge.

5.   Click on the OK button to begin the merge process.

If you chose the manual merge option, you will be presented with additional dialogs allowing you to choose the GUI Map objects that you want from the source file and move these into the target file.

Expense Calculator GUI Map File

We are now about to create a GUI Map file for the Expense Calculator using the steps that I have described above. Please refer to these steps as you repeat the process. You will need to add all 5 windows that exist in the application. Table 6.3 lists all the windows in our AUT and includes how to navigate to each window.

Window	Description	Menu Navigation
Main Window	Main application window for managing expenses.	None. Loads on application launch.
New Account	Enables you to create new accounts.	File ▶ New Account.
Open Account	Enables you to open previously created accounts.	File ▶ Open Account.
Summary	Shows you the expenses within an account, grouped by category.	Actions ▶ View Summary.
About	Provides details about the application and computer.	Help ▶ About.

Table 6.3: Windows of the Expense Calculator application.

You will notice that in the GUI Map Editor, the content of each window in your AUT is shown as being nested under the window's logical name. This is important because the window defines the context for every object that exists within it. In the next chapter when we start recording tests, you will see how WinRunner sets a window as the context window before it can reference the objects within that window.

Editing the GUI Map File

After recording a GUI Map file, it is often necessary to edit this file to modify some of the recorded properties. A few of the changes that you may want to make in your GUI Map file follow.

Modifying Logical Names

An optional, but useful step in the creation of a GUI Map file is to replace the logical names provided by WinRunner with more meaningful ones. The logical names created by WinRunner are guessed from an internal representation of an object. WinRunner's main goal is to ensure that these names are unique without being too preoccupied with finer details like length, case sensitivity or the inclusion of symbols. It is not unusual to get an object renamed something like vbedit_1 as the logical name.

The challenges posed by the default logical names provided by WinRunner includes:

- The logical names do not specify the type of object that exists.

- The logical names do not help to identify the object in your AUT.

- The logical names are difficult to reproduce because it contains symbols, spaces and special characters.

Since our goal is to simplify the process of testing, it is therefore very advisable after adding objects into your GUI Map file to rename the objects so that you solve all the problems described above. They are many useful naming conventions that you can use here, and it is often best to use the one you are most familiar with, or if you are on a team project to use the one described in the test plan. Remember that the goal of naming conventions is to promote universality among resources shared by many people. In this book, I will describe the naming convention I use. It is known as the VB Naming convention because of its popularity with the Visual Basic language. It is however, directly applicable here.

The main premise of this convention, is to name objects in the form:

objDescriptiveName

There are two parts to this, namely:

obj: A three letter prefix that specifies the generic type of the object.

DescriptiveName: A descriptive name that makes it easy to identify the object on the screen.

Notice how the first letter of every word in objDescriptiveName starts with an upper case character. This makes it easy for you to read the descriptive name portion of the object. As an example, will it be easier for you to read the following: btntodaysdate or btnTodaysDate? While btntodaysdate is not impossible to read, you have to spend a little more time determining where word boundaries end and new words begin. However, btnTodaysDate is much easier to read.

You will notice also that using this convention, you will not have to use any special characters or symbols thus making it additionally easy to reference your object names in your test script. Special characters are notoriously difficult to use in logical names and many naming conventions strongly discourage their use. Though WinRunner allows you to include special characters in logical names, The problem with this is that it becomes difficult to correctly recreate the logical name.

"<- Today's Date:" is a good example. For some, it might be difficult to see that there are 2 spaces between Today's and Date. You may also miss the fact that there is a colon after Date. WinRunner however will not miss this fact and anything you type that does not match exactly with what I have above will be considered incorrect.

Modifying Properties

The value of many properties of your object might change when your program is running. If any of these properties is a recorded property however, WinRunner will lose the ability to recognize the object. In Expense Calculator, the caption of the main window changes after each account that we open. Because this is one of the recorded properties for the object, any subsequent interaction with the main application window will result in a failure.

Updating the GUI Map

We will now look at how to change these values.

1. Open the GUI Map File in the editor.

This will allow you to choose each object and modify them individually.

2. Launch the AUT.

When the application you recorded is on screen, you can select an item in the GUI map and have WinRunner highlight the object on screen. This is a very useful feature to avoid you making changes to the wrong object.

3. Select an object in the GUI Map.

We will repeat this for each of the objects in the application. When you choose an object in the GUI Map, the actual object is highlighted in the AUT. The object has to be shown on screen for it to be highlighted. If you want to highlight the object again, click the Show button.

4. Click the Modify... button.

This opens the Modify dialog shown in Figure 6.X. Using this dialog, you can modify the logical name, or the recorded properties of each object.

5. Click the OK button.

The details about the object have now been updated in the GUI map file. You may click the Show button to verify the WinRunner still recognizes the object appropriately.

You will need to repeat this process for each of the logical names and properties that you want to change. On completion of this, you must save your GUI Map file.

Now that we have updated our GUI Map file, we will now look at how to record our test. In Chapter 7, you will see how to load your GUI Map file before you record a test. I will also show you how to merge objects into a GUI Map file.

Summary

In this chapter you have learned:

- What GUI Map files are and how they are created in WinRunner.
- The two modes that can be used in working in GUI Map files.
- How to use the GUI Map Configuration, GUI Spy, GUI Map Editor and GUI Map File Merge.
- Editing information in a recorded GUI Map object using the GUI Map editor.

CHAPTER 7

RECORDING A TEST

Now that we have created our GUI Map file, we will now begin with the creation of our tests. In this chapter we will record user operations into a test and in the next chapter I will show you how to enhance the test to verify specific functionality. To refresh your memory on the WinRunner testing process refer to Chapter 5 where I have described the WinRunner testing roadmap.

Recording Modes

In Chapter 3, I described the process of general recording/playback as it pertains to test automation tools. Briefly, it is the process where a tool (such as WinRunner) monitors what operations you perform on your computer and translates these operations into an equivalent script function. When this script is executed, it replays the operation you performed.

WinRunner supports 2 modes for recording tests. These modes are:

Context Sensitive Mode

This mode allows WinRunner to see the different GUI objects within your application as individual objects and also identify the different operations you perform on each of these objects such as click, move, select etc. WinRunner records such functions as:

```
button_press ("btnOK");
win_close ("frmExpense");
```

Notice how these TSL functions reference the names of the objects that you interacted with. This is an example of the code generated when you are recording in context sensitive mode. For most of the GUI applications you will test, you will most likely want to use the context sensitive mode.

Analog Mode

In certain applications, your mouse motions and keyboard input may be more important than the distinct objects you are performing operations on. For instance, if you are using a paint program, the motion of your mouse is important as you draw within the canvas. In this case, you want to use the analog mode for recording. This mode records the keys typed and the motion of the mouse without specifying the object it was performed on. When recording in this mode functions such as

```
move_locator_track (1);
type ("<t1>hello");
type ("<t2><kReturn>");
```
are recorded. This mode should be chosen when exact mouse movements are more important.

Within a single test, you can switch back and forth between context sensitive and analog modes of recording. This would be useful if you were working on a test case where identifying distinct objects is useful in some parts of the application and capturing mouse motion is required in other parts.

Record & Playback

The recommended process of creating tests is first to record your test based on the steps described in your test case and then to edit these recorded steps to include any checks that might be useful to the test. I will illustrate this process first by using the simple test case shown in Listing 7.1 below. This test checks that the version of the application is 1.0.#.

TIP: WinRunner provides a tool to jumpstart the test creation process. This tool, known as the RapidTest Script Wizard is discussed in Chapter 16.

```
Test Name:
       Check App Details

Purpose:
       Check that the following information about Expense
       Calculator is valid.

       a. Copyright year is 2005.
```

b. Application version information 1.0.# where the
   version info is based on the following
   1 - Major version
   0 - Minor version
   # - Build version

Pre-Conditon:
     AUT is closed.

Step	User Action	Expected Result
1	Launch the AUT	Main application window is displayed
2	Open the About page by clicking Help>>About	About dialog is displayed showing (a) Copyright year = 2005 (b) Version = 1.0.#
3	Close the About dialog by clicking the Ok button	
4	Close the AUT	

Post-Condition:
     AUT is closed.

Valid Test Data:
     N/A

Listing 7.1: Check App Details Test Case.

Prepare To Record

Before you record, you want to look closely at the test case. The main section
of the test case contains 3 columns named Step, User Action and Expected Results.
The Step column describes the numerical sequence for the actions to be
performed, the User Actions column describes the actual actions to be performed
(this is the part that we will be most concerned with in this chapter) and the
Expected Results column describes the checks we need to perform. We will use
the contents of the Expected Results column in a subsequent chapter when we
edit this test to include checkpoints.

If you look closely at the User Action column, you will notice that it contains
the operations that people using the application will perform. These are the
operations we are interested in recording. If the test case specifies any initial
condition, ensure that this condition is met before you start recording. In

addition, before you proceed with test creation, it is essential that you know the answer to the following questions:

1. Appropriate Add-ins for your AUT
2. Location of your GUI Map File
3. Recording Mode

For our test, the answers are:

1. ActiveX & Visual Basic
2. C:\MyTests\ExpenseCalculator.gui
3. Context Sensitive

Now that you have all these details you are ready to begin recording.

Recording

I will now show you the process involved in recording tests. I have broken this down into a series of steps to make it easier to replicate.

1. Select your add-in.

Launch WinRunner and ensure that you have selected the appropriate Add-in as shown in Figure 7.1. For Expense Calculator, we have selected both ActiveX Controls and Visual Basic.

Figure 7.1: The WinRunner Add-in Manager.

NOTE: If the Add-in Manager is not shown when you launch WinRunner, go to the General Options dialog and activate it. You will need to restart WinRunner after this and choose the correct add-ins.

2. Load the appropriate GUI Map.

Load the GUI Map file that contains the object mapping for this AUT by launching the GUI Map Editor and opening the GUI Map file. This loads the GUI Map into WinRunner as shown in Figure 7.2. As discussed in the previous chapter, WinRunner allows you to load several GUI map files at the same time. As stated in the previous chapter, I prefer to store all objects in the AUT into a single GUI Map file. However, for manageability in large projects it is often possible to create several smaller GUI Map files. Irrespective of whatever approach you choose to adopt, you should load all of the GUI Map files related to your AUT.

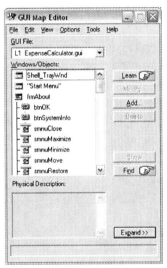

Figure 7.2: The GUI Map Editor containing the ExpenseCalculator.gui object mapping file.

After loading this, close the GUI Map Editor by clicking File ▶ Exit.

3. Start recording mode.

Enter recording mode so that WinRunner will capture your actions and translate them into TSL. You can enter recording mode by doing any of the following:

    a. Toolbar: Click on the Record Button
    b. Menu: Click Test ▶ Record – Context Sensitive
    c. Keyboard Shortcut: Press F2

The status bar will show your current recording mode by showing a recording icon and the text Ready.

CAUTION: The Record button is a switch that allows you to toggle between context-sensitive and analog modes. Check the status bar to make sure you are in the correct recording mode before proceeding.

---

4. Perform the operations in the test case.

Beginning with the first step, perform each of the operations specified in your test case. You don't need to hurry through the operation, WinRunner does not record think time, i.e. the amount of time you spend before performing operation. It is most important during this phase to get all the steps correct.

You will notice that as you perform these actions, WinRunner automatically generates TSL code into your test. These TSL statements are programmatic representations of operations you are performing and it is the reason why your company paid for WinRunner. This TSL code gives you the ability to replay the test and simulate a user manually testing the application. Listing 7.2 shows the code recorded for the test case from Listing 7.1.

```
# Shell_TrayWnd
        set_window ("Shell_TrayWnd", 6);
        button_press ("start");

# Start Menu
        set_window ("Start Menu", 2);
        list_select_item ("SysListView32_0", "Expense Calculator");

# frmExpense
        set_window ("frmExpense", 5);
        menu_select_item ("mnuHelp;mnuAbout");

# frmAbout
        set_window ("frmAbout", 3);
        button_press ("btnOK");

# frmExpense
        win_close ("frmExpense");
```

Listing 7.2: The recorded test script.

Don't worry about not understanding the code that was generated. We will discuss how to make sense of the TSL code later in the book.

5. Stop recording.

Once you have finished performing all the steps, you should instruct WinRunner to stop recording your actions. You can do this by doing any of the following:

    a. Toolbar: Click on Stop
    b. Menu: Click on Menu ▶ Stop Recording
    c. Keyboard Shortcut: Press Ctrl_L + F3

Congratulations. Your test script is now complete. You have just created your first WinRunner test. Don't forget to save your test! I have saved mine to C:\MyTests\Check App Details. This matches the test case name and makes it easy to find the test.

NOTE: Ctrl_L + F3 means pressing the left Control key and also the F3 key at the same time.

After You Record

Now that we have completed the test, we have two tasks to perform:

a. Ensure that all the objects you interacted with exist within your GUI Map.

b. Make sure the test can correctly playback your recorded operations.

We will begin by checking to see that all objects exist within our GUI Map. This is simply done by checking the temporary buffer of the GUI Map Editor to see if it contains any objects. If it does, we can selectively move the objects we interacted with into our GUI Map.

This step is only necessary if you are using the Global GUI Map file mode. You will remember that in Chapter 6, we described this mode as a format where a single GUI Map file can be shared by several tests. The other mode is the GUI Map file per test mode is a format where a GUI Map file is created for each test. In the Global GUI Map file mode, unrecognized objects are recorded into the temporary buffer where they *must* be manually moved into the GUI file (this process is described below). In the GUI Map file per test mode, unrecognized object are simply added to the GUI Map file for the test.

TIP: To check your GUI Map mode, you can select Tools ▶ General Options ▶ General from the menu.

The following steps are involved in moving all previously unrecognized objects that have been used in your test from the temporary buffer into your GUI Map file.

1. Open the GUI Map Editor.

Click on Tools ▶ GUI Map Editor.

2. Ensure you're in file mode.

Select View ▶ GUI Files from the menu.

3. Select the temporary buffer.

The temporary buffer is the first item in the list as shown in Figure 7.3.

Figure 7.3: The temporary buffer.

You will notice that the buffer contains some objects that we interacted with. These are specifically the Start Menu and Program files list. If you clear the temporary buffer without moving these objects into your GUI Map, WinRunner will not retain the knowledge of how to interact with these objects.

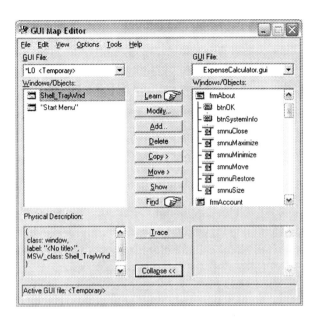

Figure 7.4: The GUI Map Editor in expanded mode.

4. Open the GUI Map Editor in expanded view.

Click the Expand >> button as shown in Figure 7.4 and select the ExpenseCalculator.gui file on the second list. Note that once the Expand >> button is clicked, the text changes to Collapse <<. This allows you to click the same button to collapse the GUI Map editor into a single list.

5. Move the objects into your map file.

Select an object from the temporary buffer list and you will see that the Move button becomes enabled. Click this button and the object is moved into your GUI Map file. Repeat for all objects in the temporary buffer that you intend to move..

6. Save and exit.

Save the changes to your GUI Map file by clicking File ▶ Save and then exit the GUI Map Editor by clicking File ▶ Exit.

Running Your Test

It is a great idea at this point to run your test simply to verify that the recorded script executes properly. To do this, we will execute our test in Debug mode. In later chapters, I will describe the entire process of test execution. At this point, we simply want to run the test to ensure that it executes properly.

1. Set the run mode to Debug Run Mode.

Select the Debug mode from the Test toolbar or the menu.

2. Run the test.

We will now run our test. You can initiate this by performing any of the following actions:

    a. Toolbar: Click From Top on the menu
    b. Menu: Click Test ▶ Run From Top
    c. Keyboard Shortcut: Press Ctrl_L + F5

This instructs WinRunner to execute your test. The test should complete execution without any errors and you can view the test results by going to Tools ▶ Test Results. Figure 7.5 shows the Test Result window after our test execution confirming that our test has run properly.

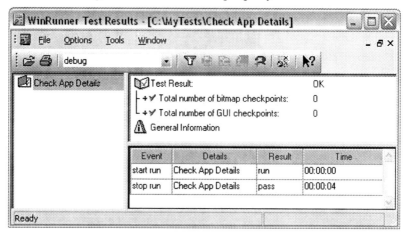

Figure 7.5: The test result window.

TIPS FOR GOOD RECORDING

1. Practice the actual actions that you intend to record. This way, you know exactly what to do.

2. Avoid performing any actions that is not listed in the test case. This could invalidate the test.

3. Close all applications that are not used for the test you are about to record.

4. Limit interactions with objects that are not in your GUI Map file. And if you do interact with these, remember to add them to your GUI Map file.

Understanding The Test

Now that we have ensured that our recorded test works properly, I will go over the recorded code line by line to help you understand what WinRunner has done. In the next chapter we will set about editing our code to include verification statements.

```
1      # Shell_TrayWnd
2              set_window ("Shell_TrayWnd", 6);
3              button_press ("start");
4
5      # Start Menu
6              set_window ("Start Menu", 2);
7              list_select_item ("SysListView32_0", "Expense Calculator");
8
9      # frmExpense
10             set_window ("frmExpense", 5);
11             menu_select_item ("mnuHelp;mnuAbout");
12
13     # frmAbout
14             set_window ("frmAbout", 3);
15             button_press ("btnOK");
16
17     # frmExpense
18             win_close ("frmExpense");
```

Listing 7.3: The recorded test script including line numbers.

TIP: You can add line numbers to the left hand column of WinRunner by choosing Tools ▶ Editor Options ▶ Options. Within this dialog, you must select both the General options ▶ Line number in gutter and the Visible gutter checkboxes.

Line 1 is a comment. Anytime WinRunner interacts with a new window, it specifies the Window name as a comment. This way you can easily find out the different windows WinRunner worked on. The window's name matches the object's logical name within your GUI Map file. Lines 5, 9, 13 and 17 are all comments also.

Line 2 shows that an operation was performed on a window called Shell_TrayWnd. This is the Window's Taskbar. Whenever you perform an object on a window, the first function that WinRunner calls is the set_window function.

This sets a window as the *context* window. Until another set_window function is called, all operations are performed on the current context window.

Line 3 clicks on the Start button in the Window's Taskbar. This is the button_press function. Notice that we did not need to specify the window that the Start button is on again. WinRunner simply uses the context window that was specified earlier using the set_window function.

Line 6 sets the Start Menu window as the context window. You should be familiar with the set_window function by now.

Line 7 clicks on the Expense Calculator item within the list of items displayed on the Start Menu dialog. The list_select_item function is specified whenever you choose (i.e. select) an item within a list. At this point, Expense Calculator launches and is displayed on the screen.

Line 8 sets the main windows of Expense Calculator as the context window. Remember that we named this window frmExpense in Chapter 6.

Line 9 selects Help ▶ About from the Expense Calculator menu. The menu_select_item is specified whenever you select an item from the menu. As you navigate through child menu, the menuitems are separated using a semicolon. So mnuHelp;mnuAbout means click on the mnuHelp object, the click on the mnuAbout child object. In our AUT, this opens up the About dialog.

Line 14 sets the About dialog as the context window using the name frmAbout from our GUI Map file.

Line 15 clicks on the OK button on this dialog effectively closing the dialog.

Line 18 closes the AUT using the win_close function. You may wonder why the set_window function was not called this time? Well, we did not interact with any objects within the window. Instead, we closed the window itself by clicking on the terminate button in the upper right hand corner of the window. If we had closed the window by clicking on File ▶ Exit, the following code would have been recorded.

```
# frmExpense
        set_window ("frmExpense", 4);
        menu_select_item ("mnuFile;mnuExit");
```

Notice that the set_window is called because we interacted with an object i.e. mnuFile within the frmExpense window.

It is clear from above that WinRunner records exactly the operation that the user performed, so the explanation of this test describes specifically the code shown in Listing 7.3. If you recorded your test by performing different operations then the test will expectedly not be the same. This is not to say that what you did is incorrect, it is simply to show that two people could create tests to test the same test case and the test would look considerably different. WinRunner simply records the exact operation performed by each person.

Summary

In this chapter you have learned:
- The different modes for recording a WinRunner test how to choose the appropriate mode for a test.

- The process involved with recording a test.

- The correct steps to take when recording a test.

- The process involved after recording a test.

- Running your test after doing a recording.

In the next chapter, we will look at how to enhance this test.

CHAPTER 8

WORKING WITH TESTS

We have just created our test and before we go farther, let us discuss some of the details about tests in WinRunner.

Editing Comments Into A Test

Before we begin including these test artifacts, I will show you how to edit your test to include comments that specify when each step from the test case starts and ends. In WinRunner, we use the # character to begin a comment. This character can be placed anywhere on a line and all words included after this character are regarded as a comment. Take a moment to look at our test case in Listing 7.1 and our recorded test in Listing 7.2.

Listing 8.1 shows the resulting code after I have merged the details from the test case into the test as comments.

```
##############################################################
# STEP 1: Launch the AUT
##############################################################
# Shell_TrayWnd
        set_window ("Shell_TrayWnd", 6);
        button_press ("start");

# Start Menu
        set_window ("Start Menu", 2);
        list_select_item ("SysListView32_0", "Expense Calculator");


##############################################################
# STEP 1: Expected result
##############################################################
```

```
###############################################################
# STEP 2: Open the About page by clicking Help->About
###############################################################
# frmExpense
        set_window ("frmExpense", 5);
        menu_select_item ("mnuHelp;mnuAbout");


###############################################################
# STEP 2: Expected result
###############################################################


###############################################################
# STEP 3: Close the About dialog by clicking the Ok button
###############################################################
# frmAbout
        set_window ("frmAbout", 3);
        button_press ("btnOK");


###############################################################
# STEP 3: Expected result
###############################################################


###############################################################
# STEP 4: Close the AUT
###############################################################
# frmExpense
        win_close ("frmExpense");


###############################################################
# STEP 4: Expected result
###############################################################
```

Listing 8.1: The Check App Details test case with included comments.

You will notice that all the lines I have included begin with a # character. This
will make the TSL interpreter ignore those lines, also, the contents I have
included show what statements form a part of steps, 1, 2, 3 & 4. Currently the
expected results section is empty and that is because we have not included any
statements to check the expected results. That is what we will do in this
chapter.
A mistake that is often made here is to assume that each line of TSL statement
makes up a step. *THIS IS WRONG!* A step is made up of one or more lines of
TSL code. Each step contains enough TSL statements to perform the operation
described by the step. It may be a little difficult for someone new to
WinRunner to know where each step starts and ends, so I will suggest

practicing with some short recording script. If you are unsure about why I have added these statements, you may want to revise the *Understanding The Test* section of Chapter 7.

NOTE: The addition of these comments is an optional step but it makes it a lot easier to identify where to add test artifacts to your code.

Now, we know exactly where to include the test artifacts in our test. Any relevant test artifact will be added to the expected results section of the appropriate step.

Anatomy Of A WinRunner Test

If you are familiar with such editing tools as Microsoft Word, you may expect that when you create a test, WinRunner generates a single file on your filesystem. But this is incorrect because, unlike your text document where all the images and items used are embedded into a single file, WinRunner tests contain several files and test artifacts that are stored separately on the filesystem. Some of these artifacts include your TSL script, data table, expected results, and stored test results. Most of these files are necessary for WinRunner to be able to load, and execute your test.

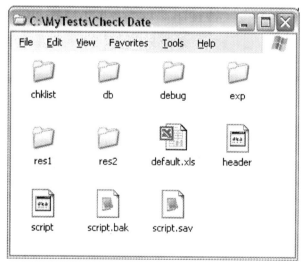

Figure 8.1: WinRunner test folder.

The first thing to note is that a WinRunner test is created on your filesystem as a folder and not as a single file. This folder contains the different test artifacts that are necessary to run a test. Even though a test is a folder, when you open the test through WinRunner, it would show up as a test. Figure 8.1 shows a folder (also a WinRunner test) containing the various test artifacts that make up the test.

In Table 8.1, I have listed some of the folders that you will find within your WinRunner test folder.

CAUTION: It is important to remember that you should not edit any of the WinRunner test artifacts outside of WinRunner. Doing so might cause irreversible damage to your test.

Name	Type	Description
chklist	Optional	Holds the entire checklist files used in your test.
db	Required	Holds important system files
debug	Required	The debug folder holding the test results whenever a test is run in debug mode. Every time a test is run in debug mode, the entire contents of this folder is overwritten.
exp	Required	The expected results folder holding the expected results for checkpoints, synchronization points etc.
res#	Optional	The results folder when the file is run in debug mode. The default format is res# where # is replaced by an incrementing number. A user can however include any name. Note that several of these folders could exist since test run results are not deleted.

Table 8.1: Folders within a WinRunner test.

Within these test folders, you will find a variety of files, included in Table 8.2 is a list of some of these files and what functionality they provide to WinRunner.

Name	Type	Description
*.xls	Optional	Contains your data table. The default name is default.xls, but you can choose any name for your data table.
default.gui	Optional	The GUI Map file name when the GUI Map Per Test mode is chosen.

header	Required	A header file containing metadata about your test.
lock	Optional	Semaphore file that contains the name of the user that has opened the WinRunner test. This file is automatically deleted once the test is closed.
script	Required	The actual script file containing your TSL code
script.bak	Required	A backup copy of your script file.
script.sav	Optional	An automatically saved copy of your script file if you have enabled the autosave option.

Table 8.2: Files found within a WinRunner test folder.

Because a test contains so many files, sending a test to someone to run does not look like an easy process. You will have to copy several files, or attach several items to the test and the recipient will have to construct the entire folder on their filesystem. Fortunately there is a much easier way. You could zip up the entire test folder and send it as a single attachment. A zip is a file archiving system that stores several files within a single file. The files are also often compressed to reduce their size and make them easier to transport through networks and mail systems.

Although several tools exist for managing zip archives that are simple to use such as Winzip (www.winzip.com) or the Compress Folder tool (in Windows XP), Mercury has made the process even easier by including a utility to zip and unzip a test from within WinRunner.

Zip a test

To export a test you are working on as a zip file, you simply need to click File ▶ Export to Zip File. Figure 8.2 shows you the dialog that you will be presented with requiring you to enter the name of your zip file.

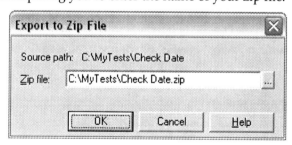

Figure 8.2: Export to Zip File dialog.

Once you click the Ok button, a zip file is generated and stored in the specified location on the filesystem.

Open a zipped test

If you receive a zipped test, you can open it up with similar ease. Simply go to File ▶ Import from Zip File and specify the location of your zip file as well as the location on your filesystem you want to import the test into. Figure 8.3 shows the dialog that you will be presented with.

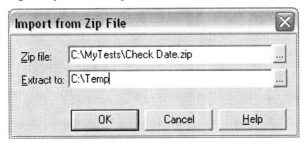

Figure 8.3: Import from Zip File dialog.

Once you click the Ok button, your test is immediately imported into the specified filesystem location and opened inside WinRunner.

External Resources

It is important to remember that a WinRunner test can also reference files that do not exist within its test folder. A GUI Map file, for example, can be located in anywhere on the filesystem and then loaded into the GUI Map editor when you want to run a test. Even the data table can be saved anywhere on the filesystem and them simply referenced from the test. Without all of these files, a test would not run properly.

Zipping a file only zips up the test folder and does not include resources external to the test folder that is being used. It is your responsibility to track these additional resources that you use in your test and then make these available to whoever wants to run your test.

TIP: By following a simple practice such as storing all your tests within a single folder on the filesystem, you can avoid having to search for your test artifacts. In this book, all our test products are stored in the C:\MyTests folder.

Test Properties

The Test Properties dialog provides you with the ability to configure your test with additional details. These details govern the add-ins loaded for the test, input parameters etc. Test properties are entered through the Test Properties dialog which can be launched clicking on File ▶ Test Properties. The dialog contains the following tabs:

General – Displays general information about the test and allows you to set some of these. Displayed details include the test name, status, filesystem location and creation date/time. Modifiable fields include the author name, test type and the name spreadsheet file to use as the data table.

Description – Allows you to specify descriptive details about the test such as the test summary description, a more extended description, and information that relates the test to requirement documents.

Parameters – Allows the definition of input parameters that allow configurable values to be passed into the test as well as output parameters that allow values to be returned from the test.

Add-ins – Provides access to choose the add-ins that will be loaded into memory when the test is opened or executed.

Current Test – Provides read-only details about the test including folder details and run mode.

Run – Allows you to specify an application or function that should be executed before your test runs. This can be useful to setup up the computer environment for test execution.

Summary

In this chapter you have learned:

- How to enhance a test script with comments relating to each step.

- The different files and folders found within a WinRunner test and what they are used for.

- How to archive a test into a single zip file and also how to open a zipped text file.

- Information about dealing with resources external to the test folder but which are used in our test.

- The Test Properties dialog and the types of information that this feature accepts.

CHAPTER 9

ENHANCING A TEST

We will now look at adding enhancements to the test that we have recorded. In the previous chapter, we went through the optional - but useful – process of adding detailed comments to our test script. We will continue this chapter with the same test. Enhancing a test allows us to go beyond record/playback functionality and actually test how the application works. We will learn how to insert test artifacts that will solve timing problems, check for expected values, and execute the test using dynamic values. The test artifacts available in WinRunner are:

Synchronization Points – Allows us to temporarily suspend execution of a test to account for timing issues in the AUT.

Data Parameterization – Allows us to use dynamic values in our test execution instead of hard-coded values.

Checkpoints – Allows us to check that certain values exist within the application at specific points in our test execution.

TSL Code – Allows us to write custom TSL statements to significantly increase the power and functionality of our tests.

It is not essential that every test contain all four of these artifacts. You only need a combination of these items that will help you perform the desired action in your test. In this, and the next few chapters we will look closely at each of these test artifacts, what function they provide, and how to insert them into our test.

Synchronization Points

With computer applications, it is difficult sometimes to determine how long it takes for certain operations to complete. Operations such as deleting a file, logging into a web application, etc. takes a variable amount of time to complete. However, in testing, it is important to know when each step finishes so that the next step can then execute. Below, I have presented a brief set of steps for viewing mail received using a generic web based email system.

1. Log in using appropriate email and password
2. Open the inbox by clicking on appropriate link
3. Click on the desired message and read it

It stands to reason that step 2 cannot be completed until step 1 finishes. At times when you log into this web application you will notice that the login process takes mere seconds, on other occasions, it takes significantly longer. Yet, it is absolutely essential that WinRunner complete step 1 before it attempts step 2. If this sequences is not followed correctly, WinRunner will incorrectly flag the test as failed. In this case, on days when the system is responding in a timely fashion, WinRunner will perform this test with no difficulties. On other days when the system takes a long time to respond, the test is failed.

Therefore, during the test creation process, it is important to identify any operation within the application that takes an unknown amount of time to complete. For these operations we will include a statement to force WinRunner to wait patiently until the operation completes. This delay is known as a synchronization point, and it can best be described using another synonym – catch-up. With synchronization points we allow the AUT's execution to catch-up to the automated testing tool's speed.

The inconsistencies in performance that we notice in our applications can be caused by many factors. It may be caused by a CPU running a different number of processes during each execution, a difference in available memory during each run, difference in the application load factor due to number of concurrent users etc. So, by inserting the synchronization point we are neutralizing this performance variance and informing WinRunner to suspend the test execution until a particular event completes. After the event occurs, WinRunner continues with test execution.

To determine if an event has occurred, we need to know if the AUT provides a visual cue or simply changes the property of a GUI object. Based on what happens, we will choose one of the two types of synchronization points available in WinRunner. These are:

Property synchronization points – Pauses execution until the property of an object attains a specific value.

Bitmap synchronization points – Pauses execution until an object or window matches a predefined visual image.

Property synchronization points

To create this synchronization point, we need three pieces of information:

1. The object that will provide the cue that the operation is complete.
2. The property belonging to this object that we will be checking.
3. The expected value the property should have from step 2.

This tells WinRunner than when the specific property (2) of the selected object (1) attains the value (3) noted, WinRunner should proceed with the test execution. Because of the possibility that the event waited for never occurs, a timeout value is also specified. If WinRunner waits until the timeout status has passed and the event has still not occurred, it makes a note in the execution log and continues with test execution. In such a scenario, there is a possibility that the test will fail because the operation being waited for had not completed.

To insert a property synchronization point in your test, use the Insert ▶ Synchronization Point ▶ For Object/Window Property.

Bitmap synchronization points

To create this synchronization point, we need to determine whether the visual cue is provided by an object, a window or a region within an object. The answer to this, determines which type of bitmap synchronization point we will create.

1. Object – If the visual cue is provided by an entire object, we will create a bitmap synchronization point by clicking Insert ▶ Synchronization Point ▶ For Object/Window Bitmap.
2. Window – When a window in the AUT provides the visual cue, we will create a bitmap synchronization point by clicking Insert ▶ Synchronization Point ▶ For Object/Window Bitmap.
3. Screen – When a region within an object provides the visual indication that an event has occurred, we use a different type of bitmap synchronization. For this, we choose the screen synchronization point by selecting Insert ▶ Synchronization Point ▶ For Screen Area. This allows us to draw a region within the object and pause until the screen image matches.

An alternate form of performing synchronization is by using the wait TSL function to pause WinRunner for a specific amount of time. The amount of time is provided in seconds and once WinRunner executes the statement, it pauses until the specified period of time passes. Meanwhile the AUT continues to execute and so can complete the current operation. Though simpler, this form of synchronization is more inefficient than the form described previously. The inefficiency results from lost time because WinRunner always waits for the specified entire time period even if the operation being waited on completes much earlier. This is correct, but what this form lacks in efficiency it makes up for in simplicity. The following statement will cause WinRunner to pause execution for 30 seconds:

```
wait(30);
```

Data-Driven Tests

After a test is created, it should not only be run only once. For many of your tests, you will want to run the tests several times using different data values for each test run. This allows you to see how your test performs with multiple data sets. It is very common for an application to work properly using one set of data and fail completely using a different set.

When you record your test, you will notice that WinRunner hard codes the values you used during the recording phase into the test script. To run the test using a different set of data, you will need to change these every time you run the test. This does not mean you have to edit the test during every execution. That is very risky because you can unintentionally introduce syntax problems into an otherwise correct test. WinRunner provides a simpler facility for this. You can parameterize the test.

Parameterizing a test means converting hard-coded data values from the test into parameters that can be read from a file. This converts your test into a data driven test. A data driven test uses test data from one or more data table. In WinRunner, the data table is a spreadsheet document and can be edited using Microsoft Excel, OpenOffice Calc or Google Spreadsheet. WinRunner also provides a Data Table editor that can conveniently be used to edit this spreadsheet.

If you are unclear about the reasons we would want to parameterize a test, please refer to Chapter 3 where I have discussed the concepts and benefits of test parameterization. In this chapter, we will look at how to parameterize our test in WinRunner.

The process of data parameterization is simple and WinRunner makes it easier still by providing a wizard to help us with the process. Parameterizing a test involves performing the following tasks:

1. Create a data table.

2. Define columns within this data table.

3. Populate the columns with data

4. Add TSL statements to your test to use the data table

TIP: It is best to perform these operations in the sequence described because each step is dependent on the previous one.

WinRunner provides the Data Driver Wizard, Parameterize Data tool and the Data Table tool that can be used for performing some, or all of these operations. You can also perform any one of the steps manually. I will go through the process of performing these steps manually, describing the process involved, then I will use the wizard and tools to perform each step.

For this exercise, I will be parameterizing the simple TSL script in Listing 9.1 that is shown below.

print("John Doe");

Listing 9.1: Simple TSL script.

On Execution, this screen pops up the WinRunner Print Log window and displays:

John Doe

The benefit of using this simple script is that it allows you to learn the concept of parameterization without worrying about your test. We will later parameterize an actual test.

Manual Test Parameterization

I will now show the process of parameterizing a test using the manual approach. I will be parameterizing the script from Listing 9.1. Note the hard coded values in bold font.

print("**John Doe**");

1. Create a data table.

To create the data table that you will use in your test navigate to Table ▶ Data Table on the menu. The first time you click on this link, a save dialog will be displayed requiring you to specify the name for your data table. Though WinRunner allows you to save a data table to any folder on the filesystem, it is recommended that you save the data table within your test folder. This makes it easier to package your test. If you save your data table in a different folder, you must remember the name of that folder and in later steps, specify the fully qualified pathname. In this example, I have named my data table *default.xls*. Once this is done, the data table (which is just a spreadsheet) is displayed on screen inside the Data Table tool. This is shown in Figure 9.1.

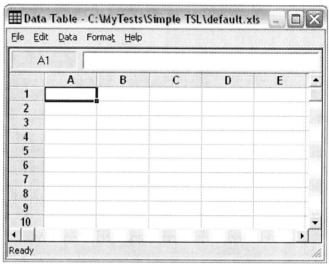

Figure 9.1: The empty data table.

2. Add columns to the data table.

To specify a column, double click the header of the column. By default, the data table columns are named A, B, C, D etc. You cannot use these column names and must define yours. Also it is very important to remember that columns are case sensitive.

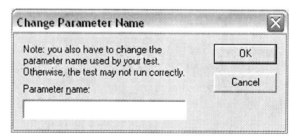

Figure 9.2: Dialog to change a column name in the data table.

Figure 9.2 shows the dialog that is displayed when you double click the header column of the data table. Click OK once you have entered an acceptable name. In this example, I have created a column named datName.

82

3. Add data to the column.

This step is similar to working on a standard spreadsheet document. The data table provides you with the ability to import data from a data source such as a database, import a CSV file, paste in data from another document etc. In our case, I will go the boring route of simply typing in the data I need.

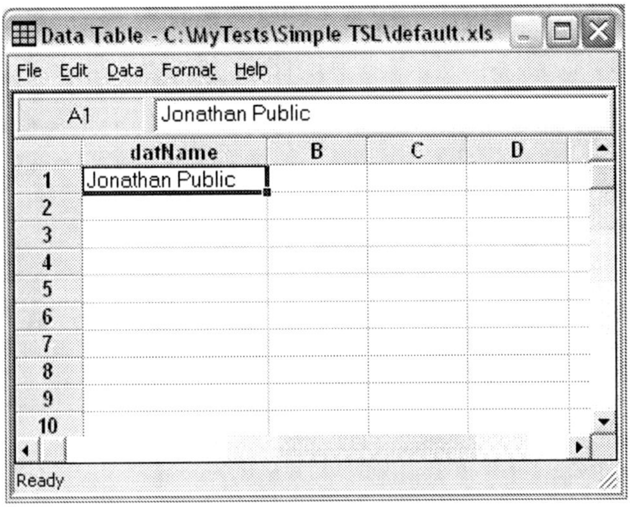

Figure 9.3: The data table with data entered.

TIP: In spreadsheets, numbers cannot have leading zeros. So, to enter an item such as 02.15 and preserve the leading zero, you must type in '02.15 into the column.

---

4. Save your changes.

Click File ▶ Save on the Data Table tool's menu to save the data you entered. Your data cannot be used until the file is saved.

5. Use TSL to iterate through the data table.

The statements I have included here are the same statements that the Data Driver Wizard will include. What these TSL statements do is to identify the data table file, open it and loop through the contents.

```
table = "default.xls";
rc = ddt_open(table, DDT_MODE_READ);
if (rc!= E_OK && rc != E_FILE_OPEN)
        pause("Cannot open table.");
ddt_get_row_count(table,table_RowCount);
for(table_Row = 1; table_Row <= table_RowCount; table_Row ++)
```

83

```
{
        ddt_set_row(table,table_Row);
        print("John Doe");
}
ddt_close(table);
```

Listing 9.2: TSL code for creating a data driven test.

6. Use TSL to replace hard-coded values with values from the data table.

We would now replace the print("John Doe"); with print(ddt_val(table, "datName"));
Notice that the added code reads values from the column titled datName and
prints the value displayed in that column. The final resulting TSL code is
displayed in Listing 9.3.

```
1       table = "default.xls";
2       rc = ddt_open(table, DDT_MODE_READ);
3       if (rc!= E_OK && rc != E_FILE_OPEN)
4               pause("Cannot open table.");
5       ddt_get_row_count(table,table_RowCount);
6       for(table_Row = 1; table_Row <= table_RowCount; table_Row ++)
7       {
8               ddt_set_row(table,table_Row);
9               print(ddt_val(table, "datName"));
10      }
11      ddt_close(table);
```

Listing 9.3: Completed data driven test.

If we run this code, it will launch the WinRunner Print Log and display the
value:

Jonathan Public

Understanding The Test

This is all that is needed to create a data driven test. Remember that the
numbers are not included as part of the TSL statements. I have simply added
them here so that we can discuss the code created.

Line 1 assigns the data table to a variable called table. Notice that we used the
name default.xls, which is what we named the data table in step 1. If you stored
the data table in a location different than the test folder, you must specify the
fully qualified pathname here.

Line 2 uses the ddt_open() function to open the file for reading. The result of this operation is stored in a variable named rc.

Line 3 checks the value of the rc variable to see if we succeeded opening the file. If there was any error during the opening, a message is displayed in Line 4.

Line 5 uses the ddt_get_row_count() function to get the number of rows in the data table (we use the table variable). This count is stored in a variable named table_RowCount.

Line 6 initiates a loop allowing us to run this code for every line in the data table file. A new variable table_Row is created, starting from 1 and loops until it gets to the number of rows in the file denoted by table_RowCount. To change the number of times this loop runs you want to change the stopping condition from Line 6 highlighted in bold font.

```
for(table_Row = 1; table_Row <= table_RowCount; table_Row ++)
```

This loop repeats for operations defined at Line 8 and Line 9.

Line 8 uses the ddt_set_row() function to set the current row within the data table that we intend to read from. It uses the table variable to specify the data table we are using and the table_Row variable to specify what row we want to read.

Line 9 uses the ddt_val() function to get the value of the datName column from out data table. Remember that our hard coded value is replaced by a call to this function. So, we can say that the hard-coded value has been replaced by a parameter.

Line 11 closes the data table. This is good house-keeping since we are now done with the file. It frees the resource for any other process that might need to use the file.

Automated Test Parameterization

I will now show how to repeat this process using the tools provided by WinRunner. The simple TSL test being parameterized is the same as I used in the manual parameterization process. This test is shown in Listing 9.1.

1. Create a data table and TSL statements to the test.

This is done using the Data Driver Wizard. First, we will highlight the code we intend to parameterized and launch the Data Driver Wizard by clicking Table ▶ Data Driver Wizard on the menu. Figure 9.4 shows the dialog that is displayed. This simply provides us with information about what the wizard can do. Click on Next to begin using the wizard and the dialog in Figure 9.5 is displayed.

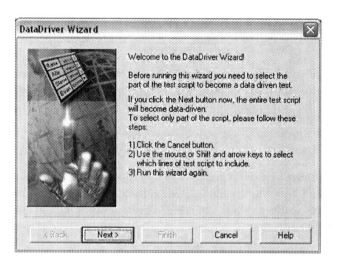

Figure 9.4: Initial page of the Data Driver Wizard.

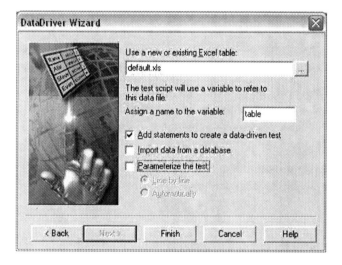

Figure 9.5: Continuation page of the Data Driver Wizard.

Notice that we have specified the name for out data table as default.xls in this wizard. We have also chosen a variable named table to use to reference our data table in the TSL code that is generated. Finally we have asked the wizard to generate TSL statements to parameterize our test.

We are asking this wizard to perform multiple tasks for us and when we click the Finish button, the following code is generated.

```
table = "default.xls";
rc = ddt_open(table, DDT_MODE_READ);
if (rc!= E_OK && rc != E_FILE_OPEN)
        pause("Cannot open table.");
```

```
ddt_get_row_count(table,table_RowCount);
for(table_Row = 1; table_Row <= table_RowCount; table_Row ++)
{
        ddt_set_row(table,table_Row);
        print("John Doe");
}
ddt_close(table);
```

Notice that this is exactly the same code that we typed in Listing 9.2.

2. Define columns, populate with data and reference the column.

For this, we will use the Parameterize Data tool. To begin, highlight the value
you want to replace with a parameter. In our case, we will highlight the word
"John Doe". Make sure to include the double quotes. Next we will invoke the
Parameterize Data tool by navigating to Table ▶ Parameterize Data on the
menu. The image displayed in Figure 9.6 is shown.

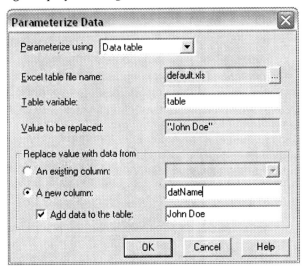

Figure 9.6: The Parameterize Data dialog.

Notice the values pre-filled for the Excel table file name, table variable and
value to be replaced. You want to ensure that these values are correct from
your test. Finally, we have specified a new column to replace our data value
from and named this column datName. This dialog also adds the value John Doe
to the data table.

Figure 9.7 shows the data table after this step is completed.

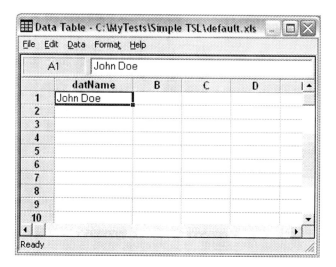

Figure 9.7: The Data Table after parametrizing the test above.

You can now change this data table value and the value would be used in your test. The code that is generated after this step is shown below. Again note that it is identical to the code I created in Listing 9.3.

We now have a fully parameterized test. To under stand the TSL code, look at the **Understanding The Test** section created previously in this chapter.

Summary

In this chapter you have learned:

- How to enhance a test script with comments relating to each step.

- The different test artifacts that can be added to a TSL test.

- What a synchronization point is, and how to include one in the test.

- What data parameterization is, and how to parameterize a test.

CHAPTER 10

CHECKPOINTS

Checkpoints are undoubtedly the most important feature in automated testing. They provide us with a way to verify that the application produces the results we expect it to produce. If you click the Today's date button on Expense Calculator for instance, you would expect the correct system date to be displayed in the field. To verify that this actually happened we need to use a checkpoint.

Keep in mind that we write tests for unattended execution, so when we run our tests, we are not available to visually verify that the expected results were met. In this chapter, we will examine the different types of checkpoints that exist in QTP.

The Checkpoint process

The greatest thing about checkpoints is the simplicity of implementation. We can use most of the checkpoints that WinRunner provides in a simple three-step process. Most of these checkpoints can be implemented without writing any TSL code. The three steps that are involved in working with a checkpoint are:

Step 1: During the creation of our test script, we create a checkpoint. This establishes the *expected result* of the checkpoint.

Step 2: During the test execution, WinRunner gets the *actual result* from the application environment.

Step 3: WinRunner compare the *expected result* and the *actual result*. If they match, WinRunner **passes** the step. If they do not match, WinRunner **fails** the step.

We only have to worry about creating the checkpoint (step 1 from above). WinRunner handles the subsequent steps during execution. There are 4 types of items we can check using checkpoints.

GUI Checkpoint – This checks whether the properties of an object has the value we expect it to have.

Bitmap Checkpoint – This compares an object on screen with a previously captured snapshot.

Database Checkpoint – Allows you to compare values from a database captured during runtime against a set of value captured during test creation.

Text Checkpoint – Compares the text displayed within an object with a previously captured text value.

We will now look closely how to create each of these different checkpoints.

GUI Checkpoints

GUI checkpoints are used too check expected results for GUI objects. This checkpoint allows us to determine whether specific operations have occurred within the AUT. You can use this to determine such functionalities as whether an object has focus or whether an object is enabled.

WinRunner supports three different types of GUI checkpoints. These are:

Single Property – This GUI checkpoint checks a single property of a single object. It is the easiest checkpoint to create because it inserts a single TSL statement in your code and does not create a checklist.

Object/Window – This checks one or more properties of an object/window. The checkpoint creates a checklist, which is a list of properties that will be checked at run time.

Multiple Objects – This checkpoint is used to check one or more properties of one or more objects. This is similar to creating several object/window checkpoints but it is much more convenient.

Although there are three checkpoint types, one of them (the single property checkpoint) inserts a single TSL statement in a code, and the Object/Window and Multiple Objects checkpoints create a checklist.

Single Property GUI Checkpoint

This is the simplest checkpoint to create and it checks the value of a single object property. You can create a single property GUI checkpoint using the following process.

Before you begin, ensure that your cursor is in the position in your test where you want to insert the checkpoint. Also, ensure that your AUT is launched and the GUI object you wish to check is displayed on screen.

1. Select the single property GUI checkpoint from the menu.

Click on Insert ▶ GUI Checkpoint ▶ For Single Property from the menu. This will convert your cursor to a pointer.

2. Click on the object you want to check.

This selects the object and displays the Check Property dialog as shown in Figure 10.1.

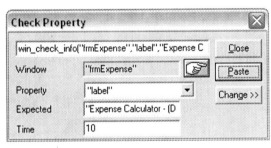

Figure 10.1: The Check Property dialog.

If you clicked on the wrong object, you can click on the pointer shown in the dialog and click on the correct object again.

3. Modify the checkpoint details.

Enter the following information in the Check Property dialog.
- Properties – Select the property you want to check.
- Expected – Modify this to the value you expect.
- Time – Specify the maximum amount of time you are willing to wait for the event to occur.

4. Click on the Paste button.

This inserts the TSL statement for the checkpoint into your code. The TSL code below verifies that the AUT window is displayed as required in the expected results of step 1.

```
win_check_info("frmExpense","label","Expense Calculator - (Default)",10);
```

Object/Window GUI Checkpoint

This checkpoint works similarly to a single property checkpoint except that it checks multiple properties of a single object. For this, it creates a checklist which is a list of properties of an object which it intends to check.

The following steps are used to create an Object/Window GUI checkpoint.

1. Select the object/window GUI checkpoint from the menu.

Click on Insert ▶ GUI Checkpoint ▶ For Object/Window from the menu. This will convert your cursor to a pointer.

2. Click on the object you want to check.

This selects the object and inserts a TSL statement into the test. The code below is the statement it included.

```
win_check_gui("frmExpense", "list3.ckl", "gui3", 1);
```

3. Modify the checkpoint details.

Edit the checklist by selecting Insert ▶ Edit GUI Checklist from the menu. From the list displayed, choose the appropriate checklist. From the statement above, the checklist we want is list3.ckl.

Figure 10.2: The Open Checklist dialog.

You will notice that the checklist we want is included in the list. If you choose this checklist and click on Ok, the checklist opens in the Checklist editor allowing you to choose the new properties you want to check.

4. Save the modified checkpoint.

Click the OK button and overwrite the existing checkpoint with the new details.

Multiple Objects GUI Checkpoint

This checkpoint is very similar to the Object/Window GUI Checkpoint. The difference here is that it allows you to check properties for multiple objects. When you select this checkpoint by clicking Insert ▶ GUI Checkpoint ▶ Multiple Objects from the WinRunner menu, it displays the Checklist Editor shown in Figure 10.3. Using this editor, you can add all the objects you want to check and select the properties you are interested in checking.

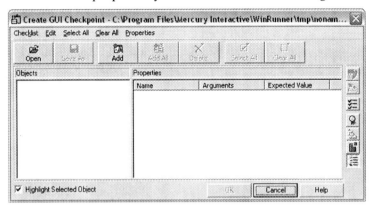

Figure 10.3: The Checklist editor.

Database Checkpoints

A database checkpoint is another type of checkpoint supported by WinRunner. This checkpoint allows us to verify that the data our AUT reads from and writes to the database is correct.

To use database checkpoints, there are two technologies you need to be familiar with. The first is SQL, a standardized language used for retrieving information from a database. In a database checkpoint, WinRunner only allows you to use the SQL SELECT statement. This statement simply does data retrieval without modifying the database. All the other types of SQL statements modify the structure or contents of the database. We cannot use any of these other statements for a database checkpoint in WinRunner.

Another technology that is important to understand is ODBC. This is a technology that allows you to connect your computer to a database so that WinRunner can retrieve data from the database.

The developers of WinRunner cannot know what type of database your AUT uses, so it is impossible for WinRunner to know how to connect to your database. Without being able to connect to your database however, all database checkpoints will fail. SO, what can be done? WinRunner was created with built in support for ODBC. You can then teach ODBC how to connect to your database.

Since WinRunner can connect to ODBC, and you've taught ODBC how to connect to your database, it stands to reason that WinRunner can now connect to your database. We will now look at how WinRunner deals with ODBC.

Understanding ODBC

The concept of ODBC is important for database connectivity because it provides a way in which the application developer can insulate themselves from the inherent difficulties in learning how to connect to every possible type of database that exists. Using ODBC, the developer simply connects to an ODBC data source and lets the ODBC connection specify the database it wants to connect to.

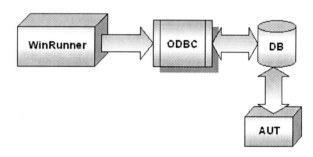

Figure 10.4: Indirect connection to a database using ODBC.

This means that to use ODBC during your testing, you will need to create an ODBC data source. We will now go through the process of creating this. Before we create an ODBC data source we need to know at least three details, including:

Data Source Name - A unique data source name (DSN) that you will use to refer to your database on the machine. Think of the DSN as an alias for the database. While the DSN can really be anything, it is often best to specify a name that bears some relation to the real database, or the AUT.

CAUTION: Don't forget that you must create the same DSN on all machines you intend to run your test on. Without doing so, your test will not have a valid connection to the database and as such, will fail.

Data Source Type - The type of data source which you intend to create. There are two major types:

- Machine data source
- File data source

Database Driver installed - You can only create an ODBC data source for a database that has the appropriate drivers installed on your system. You can easily check the list of drivers you have installed by clicking on the Drivers tab of the ODBC dialog.

You will find that the choice of drivers chosen determines the type of details that will be requested from you during the process of adding your data source. Access, for instance being a file based database provides a button that allows you to select the database file from the filesystem while SQL Server, a connection based database, request such details as the host on which the database is running. Expectedly, you cannot conclude the creation of an ODBC data source if you do not have all the necessary details.

Bitmap Checkpoints

These checkpoints are used to compare two images during test execution. Bitmap checkpoints should be used carefully because they are susceptible to false negatives such as:

- Window decorations – These are the type of window elements that exist in each operating system. The window decorations of Windows 98 differ from Windows XP, Windows Vista etc. and so a bitmap checkpoint created on a Windows 98 machine may fail in a Windows XP machine simply because the windows look different.

- Screen Resolution – Running a bitmap checkpoint on a machine other than the machine the checkpoint was create for could result in false positives if the screen resolution o both machines do not match. A bitmap checkpoint merely compares two images without making adjustments for screen resolutions.

- Color Settings - Usage of a different color setting on different machines could also result in errors. This difference may be due to a limitation in capabilities of one of the systems such as a less powerful video card etc.

Because of these limitations, you should use a bitmap checkpoint only when other checkpoints are not possible for what is being checked. For instance, you need to verify the color of an object.

The process of creating a bitmap checkpoint is simple and I use this to verify the copyright information from the test in Listing 7.1.

1. Select the bitmap checkpoint from the menu.

Click on Insert ▶ Bitmap Checkpoint and choose either For Object/Window or For Screen Area. For our checkpoint, we are using the For Screen Area because we only want to check a portion of the contents of the About dialog. We are only interested in the copyright information.

2. Draw the region on the object you want to check.

Using the cursor, draw a rectangular region you want to create a bitmap checkpoint of on the object. A highlighted region will appear as shown in Figure 10.5.

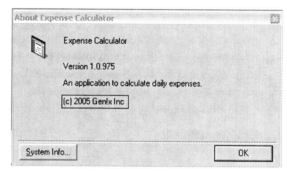

Figure 10.5: The About dialog showing a bitmap checkpoint area.

If you selected the wrong region, simply redraw the region. Once you are satisfied with the result, right click and WinRunner inserts the TSL statement below into your test.

win_check_bitmap("frmAbout", "Img2", 1, 70, 120, 93, 16);

Notice that in this win_check_bitmap function, it specifies the object name, as the first argument and image name as the second argument. This image name is the image captured during this step and stored internally by WinRunner as the expected result. The last four arguments are the coordinates on the screen matching the region you drew.

Text Checkpoint

A text checkpoint is different from all the other types of checkpoints that we have seen so far. It simply creates a TSL function that captures the runtime value of text that is displayed within an object or screen area.

You will remember from the introduction section of this chapter that to create a proper checkpoint, you need to compare this captured value to an expected result. It is this comparison that determines whether the test passed or failed.

For text checkpoints, this comparison must be added by manually writing the appropriate TSL code. As an example, one of our checkpoints is verifying that the About dialog, displayed in Figure 10.6, always shows Version 1.0.# as the version of the application. To check this, we will insert a text checkpoint to capture the text in the window and then write TSL code to perform the comparison.

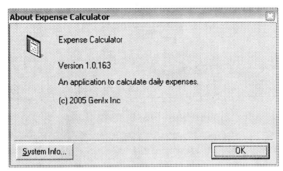

Figure 10.6: The About dialog.

I will show how to do this using the following steps.

1. Select the text checkpoint from the menu.

Click on Insert ▶ Get Text and choose either For Object/Window or For Screen Area. For our checkpoint, we are using the For Object/Window menuitem. Your cursor immediately becomes a pointer.

2. Click on the object you want to check.

This selects the object and inserts a TSL statement into your code. The code inserted is:

win_get_text("frmAbout", text);

This TSL function simply captures the text from the About dialog of the Expense Calculator application and stores it into a variable named text.

3. Write the TSL code to perform the check.

This selects the object and inserts a TSL statement into your code. The

TSL code below checks the version information.

```
win_get_text("frmAbout", text);
if ( index(text, "Version 1.0.") > 0 ) {
    tl_step("Step 2", 0, "The version information is correct");
    pause(index(text, "Version 1.0."));
} else {
    tl_step("Step 2", 1, "The version information is WRONG!");
}
```

Listing 10.1: Code for a text checkpoint.

The TSL statements used in this listing simply scans the text for a string with the value Version 1.0., if this is found, it writes a pass statement to the test results window using the tl_step function. If the statement is not found, it uses another tl_step statement to write a fail statement.

In the next chapter, you will learn the TSL script language and become familiar with how to use this in your tests.

More on Checkpoints

If you have used other Mercury tools such as QuickTest Professional, you may find that the capacity to modify the expected results in WinRunner for both the GUI checkpoint (except Single property) and Database checkpoint is quite limited. The expected results of these two checkpoints are set simply by running your test in Update Run Mode and are not directly modifiable by the user.

To get around this, you may choose to script your own checkpoint statements. TSL provides the obj_get_info function which you can use to get any property of an object as well as the ability to execute a SQL statement against a database. Using this type of checkpoint is clearly more powerful as you have the ability to determine what expected results you are checking for. However, it does require a good understanding of TSL.

Make sure you pay attention to the TSL language in the next chapter.

Editing Checklists

The creation of certain GUI and Database checkpoints creates a checklist within your test folder. You can easily modify the contents of a checklist by selecting Insert ▶ Edit GUI Checklist, Insert ▶ Edit Database Checklist or Insert ▶ Edit Runtime Record Checklist from the menu. Figure 10.7 shows the dialog you are provided with. Note that this dialog contains your previously created checklist. Selecting this checklist and clicking on the Ok button launches the Checklist editor for the type of checklist you selected. All modifications to a checklist must be done within the checklist editor.

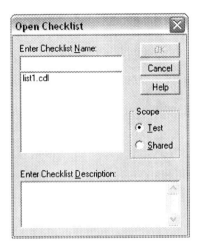

Figure 10.7: The Open Checklist dialog.

TIP: After modifying a checklist, you should run your test in Update Run Mode to update the expected results of your checkpoint. In Chapter 13 I have described this run mode in detail.

Summary

In this chapter, we have looked at the various types of checkpoints that exist in WinRunner and described how to create each of them. The checkpoints that we have looked at include GUI, bitmap, database and text checkpoints. We have also looked at how to use the Update Run Mode to update the expected results of each checkpoint.

CHAPTER 11

TEST SCRIPT LANGUAGE

We will now look at the TSL language. You have already been exposed to this language on many occasions in this book. All the recorded scripts that WinRunner creates when you perform an operation is in TSL code syntax. Keep in mind that while mastery of TSL is not required for creating automated tests, knowledge of the language helps to enhance the recorded tests and to make your tests highly sophisticated. Skillful usage of TSL can help limit the need for manual intervention when running your test and additionally make your test less error-prone.

Test Script Language

TSL is the script language used by WinRunner for recording and executing scripts. In this chapter, I will provide you with the foundational concepts of TSL. Think of these as the building blocks of TSL scripting that will help you learn how to write the language. Another useful resource to review while learning TSL is the WinRunner help system.

TIP: To access the WinRunner help system at any time, press the F1 key.

The TSL language is very compact containing only a small number of operators and keywords. If you are proficient in any programming language, you will find TSL easy to learn. In fact, you will find it much easier than learning a programming language because TSL is a script language. Script languages do not have many of the complex syntax structures you may find in programming languages. On the other hand, TSL being a script language has considerably less features and capabilities than a programming language.

Table 11.1 shows the list of features that are available in TSL.

Feature	Description
Comments	Allows users to enter human readable information into the test script. The interpreter will ignore these statements.
Naming Rules	Rules for creating identifiers within TSL.
Datatypes	The different types of data values that are supported by the language.
Data Storage	Containers that can be used to store information.
Operations	Different type of computational operations.
Branching	Avoids executing certain portions of the code unless a condition is met.
Loops	Repeats execution of a certain section of code.
Functions	Group of statements used to perform some useful functionality.

Table 11.1: Parts of the TSL Language.

History

TSL stands for Test Script Language and is often referred to by its acronym. Created by Mercury Interactive an used in several of their product line including WinRunner, XRunner and LoadRunner, TSL has similarities in functionality and keywords to the C language and any of its derivatives. Knowledge of similar languages as JavaScript, Perl or Java would aid in your quick understanding of TSL.

General Syntax Rules

1. Semi-colons mark the end of a simple statement.

You may have seen that many of the recorded statements in your test ends with a semicolon. This is important because TSL, like other C-based languages use the semi-colon to specify the end of a statement much like you would use a period to specify the end of a sentence in English. The following code:

```
foo();
bar();
```

can then be written as:

foo(); bar();

and WinRunner will still execute them properly.

2. Compound statements use curly braces and not semi-colons.

Compound statements, i.e. statements that can hold other statements within them do not end with a semi-colon. So, the if statement, which is a compound statement is written as:

```
if ( 1 > 0 ) {
  foo();
}
```

Notice that the content within the if statement has the semi-colon and not the if statement itself. It would be WRONG to write the if statement in the following form:

```
if ( 1 > 0 ); {
  foo();
}
```

3. TSL is case-sensitive.

TSL is a case-sensitive language so pay special attention to the case of the statements that you write. Most of the identifiers, operators and functions within the language utilize lower case. So, when you are unsure, try lower case.

TIP: When writing compound statements, it is highly beneficial to indent the content of the compound statement. This makes it easier to identify the code that is a part of the statement. Though the interpreter does not care about indentation, indented code is easier for you to read.

We will now look closely at the different parts of the TSL language. I have listed these in Table 11.1.

Comments

The first part of the TSL language that we will look at is comments. Comments allow you to include human-language statements within a TSL test and have these statements ignored by the interpreter. These inserted comments are useful because they provide the reader of the test script with useful information about the test. To create a comment, type the # symbol anywhere on a line. Every statement that appears after this symbol is regarded as a comment. The # symbol can appear as the first character in a line making the whole line a comment, or anywhere in the line creating a partial line comment. e.g.

\# This is a whole line comment

foo(); \# This is a partial line comment

NOTE: When a comment is specified, the font style and color in the editor changes. You can control how the font looks for comments as well as for several other items in the editor by clicking on Tools ▶ Editor Options.

Unlike some other languages that you may be used to, TSL does not have multi-line comments. You will have to place the # character at the start of each line you wish to convert into a comment.

TIP: It is a good idea to use comments liberally in your test to make it easier for people to understand the assumptions/decisions you made in the test.

Naming Rules

Every language has rules that define what names are acceptable in the language and what names are not. In TSL, several items have to be given names including variables, constants and functions. These names are the identifiers that we use to refer to the item. The following rules are used for naming identifiers in TSL.

1. *Must begin with a letter or the underscore* - Names like count, strInfo, _data are acceptable but names like 2day, 4get, *count violate this rule.

2. *Cannot contain special characters except the underscore* - Names can only be made up of alphabets, numbers and the underscore. Symbols and other special characters are not allowed.

3. *Cannot match a reserved word* - Words having special meanings to TSL cannot be used as variable names, so names like for, if, in etc. are not allowed.

4. *Must be unique within a context* - This prevents you from giving two items the same name at the same time. Why would you want to avoid this? Well, for the same reasons you avoid given two children in the same house, the same name.

5. *Are case-sensitive* - Meaning that you can declare foo, Foo, and FOO as three different named items without violating rule 4. Be careful if you choose to do this though, our minds don't generally think in case-sensitive terms.

In Chapter 6, I described a naming convention that can be used in renaming GUI map objects. The same convention is very applicable here. By naming variables using prefixes of num and str to denote numbers and strings, you can create variables that are easy to remember and non-confusing.

Datatypes

Every script language has different types of data that can be stored during the script's execution. These different types of data are known as datatypes. While some languages have several datatypes, TSL has only two. The two datatypes available in TSL are:

String - for storing alphanumeric data. Strings are denoted by putting double quotes (") around values. Examples include "Hello", "John Q. Public", "101 Curl Drive", "It was the best of times, it was the worst..."

Number - for storing numeric data. Numbers can have negative values, hold decimal places, or be denoted in exponential notation. Examples include 21, -6, 12.31, -4e5, and 4E-5.

Although there are two datatypes, we do not need to specify the type of a variable during creation. TSL simply uses the context in which we access the data to determine what the datatype is. Information is converted easily and flexibly between both types. The following code:

```
foo = "2" + 1;
```

results in foo being assigned the numeric value 3 because TSL sees this as an arithmetic operation and converts the string appropriately to a number. However, the following code:

```
bar = "2" & 1;
```

results in bar being assigned the string value "21". The difference here is that when & (string concatenation) is used, a string operation is performed and the operands are converted to string. However, when + (addition) is used, the operands are converted to numbers and an arithmetic operation is performed. We will take a closer look at these different TSL operators later.

ESCAPE SEQUENCES

Strings are alphanumeric values enclosed in double quotes e.g.

foo = "Hello";

would hold the value *Hello*. But what if you want to store the value *John "Q" Public*? To do this, you have to write the code:

foo = "John \"Q\" Public";

Note that we have included a backslash (\) in front of the double quote. This format allows us to store the literal value of the double quote. This is known as using an escape sequence and it is a way to include certain types of characters and values within a string. TSL defines other escape sequences and I have included these in Table 11.2 below.

Feature	Description
\"	Double quote
\\	Backslash
\b	Backspace
\n	New line
\number	Storing octal numbers e.g. \8 is 10 in decimal notation
\t	Horizontal tab
\v	Vertical tab

Table 11.2: TSL escape sequences.

When you are referring to file names on a computer, pay careful attention to escape sequences. Referring to the file:

C:\newfile.txt

Will be interpreted by the system as

C:
ewfile.txt

You may notice that the system converted the \n to a newline statement. To prevent this, you will need to escape the \ (i.e. the path delimiter). So, you must use the \\ sequence instead. This means the file name will be written as:

C:\\newfile.txt

This is a very important item to remember and you will see the usage of \\ in all instances where I refer to a file.

Data Storage

This refers to how information is stored in the test during execution. Computers need to store large amounts of data during test execution. These include:

- dynamic values - values that can change

- fixed values - values that remain the same through test execution

- sets - groups of values.

TSL uses three different types of storage vehicles. These include variables - for dynamic storage, constants - for fixed values and arrays - for sets. Each of the storage devices are described below:

Variables - Containers that can hold a piece of information. The information being held can be changed over the lifetime of the variable.

Constants - Containers that can hold a piece of information. The information being held cannot be changed.

Arrays - A single container that can be used to hold several pieces of information at the same time. This is used to hold information that are related e.g. names of people, states etc.

Data storage only refers to information that needs to be stored temporarily during test execution. For information that you want to store permanently, you should consider writing to a file or database.

Variables

In our code, we often need to temporarily store information that we plan to use later. This is similar to when someone tells you a phone number. You may write this phone number down to later use. The piece of paper you wrote the number on is a storage device for the information. Just as you can erase the value on the paper and write a new piece of information, you can similarly change the value in a variable. So, for the multiple pieces of information that your test script will collect and process you will need variables to hold them.

In many programming languages, a variable must be declared before use. But in TSL, variable declaration is optional so you can create a variable simply by using the variable in your code. Whenever the interpreter comes across a new variable being used in your code, it automatically handles the declaration for you. This is known as implicit declaration. The only exception to this rule is in functions (discussed later in this chapter) where variable declaration is required.

Declaring a variable is done using the following form:

class variable [= value];

Meaning that you either write

class variable;

106

or

class variable = value;

The first form simply declares the variable while the second form initializes it with a value.

The word class should be replaced with a value from Table 11.3 below and variable is any name that conforms to all the naming rules I have listed earlier.

Class	Scope	Use in function	Use in test
auto	Local	Yes	No
extern	Global	Yes	Yes
public	Global	No	Yes
static	Local	Yes	Yes

Table 11.3: Class values for variable declaration.

The following example declares a static variable named numCount and assigns it a value of 7.

static numCount = 7;

Constants

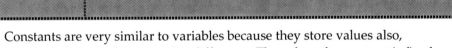

Constants are very similar to variables because they store values also, however, they also have a major difference. The value of a constant is fixed and cannot be changed during code execution. Constants are typically used when an item being described has a fixed value in the real world. E.g.

const DAYS_IN_WEEK = 7;

This way, instead of writing:

foo = 30 / 7;

whenever you are doing date based calculations, you can write:

foo = 30 / DAY_IN_WEEK;

The difference is subtle but ultimately the second form of the code is a little easier to read. Additionally, if you need to change the calculation of days from calendars days (7) to business days (5), you can easily change this in the constant declaration and have the change propagate throughout your entire code.

Arrays

Sometimes you may want to store several pieces of related data such as names. One way to do this is to declare different variables for each value e.g.

```
name1 = "John";
name2 = "Jane";
name3 = "Joe";
```

While this would work adequately for your needs, TSL provides a better mechanism for use when dealing with a collection of similar items. This concept, known as arrays, allows you to store several values of related information into the same variable. Each value must be stored within a different index in the variable name. So, the code written above can be rewritten as:

```
names[0] = "John";
names[1] = "Jane";
names[2] = "Joe";
```

The [ ] indicates that you are storing information into an array and the number specifies the appropriate index. Indeed, the code looks very similar to what we wrote previously. So, you might ask, what is the benefit of an array? The answer is that using an array, I can easily perform operations on my entire collection of names without having to deal with multiple variables. I can use TSL constructs such as loops to perform operations on the entire array quite easily. The following code:

```
for (i=0; i<3; i++) {
  print(names[i]);
}
```

prints out the three names in my array. If the array had 50 separate values, I would still use a similarly compact amount of code to print all the values. I would just need to change the range of values that I am instructing the loop to use. If I used 50 different variables, the amount of code I would need to write to print each name would be far greater.

When working with arrays, there are a few rules to remember.

1. Arrays are declared using the following rules:

```
class array[] [ = initialization ];
```

where class is a variable declaration type (see Table 11.3), array is valid name (see Naming Rules), and initialization is a set of initial values. Notice that in this construct, the initialization is optional so I can declare an array as:

```
public names[] = {"John", "Jane", "Joe" };
```

or

```
public names[];
```

2. Arrays can be initialized in 2 ways. Using standard initialization shown below:

```
public names[] = {"John", "Jane", "Joe" };
```

or by using an explicit form of initialization such as:

```
public names[];
names[0] = "John";
names[1] = "Jane";
names[2] = "Joe";
```

3. TSL supports associative arrays allowing you to use strings as your array indexes. For instance:

```
capital["Ohio"] = "Columbus";
```

is valid TSL code that stores *Columbus* within the array capital at the index *Ohio*.

4. Array indexes do not have to start from 0. As shown above, the indexes do not even have to be numbers at all.

5. Arrays can be multidimensional allowing you to store multiple pieces of information at each index. The following code:

```
names["first", 1] = "John";
names["first", 2] = "Jane";
names["middle", 1] = "Q";
names["middle", 2] = "";
names["last", 1] = "Public";
names["last", 2] = "Doe";
```

generates data that can be displayed in the following form shown in Table 11.4.

names	1	2
first	John	Jane
middle	Q	
last	Public	Doe

Table 11.4: The 2-dimensional names array.

A 1-dimensional array can be represented as a list, a 2-dimensional array can be represented as a table and a 3-dimensional array can be drawn as a cube. While TSL supports arrays with 4 or more dimensions, it is often more difficult to conceptualize these and their usage are therefore not recommended.

109

Operations

Operations are the many forms of computations, comparisons etc. that can be performed in TSL. The symbols used in an operation are known as operators and the values involved in these operations are known as operands. Most of the operations in TSL are binary operations, meaning they involve two operands. Two of the operations are unary (i.e. involving a single operand), and one operation is tertiary (i.e. involving three operands).

For unary operations, the syntax is in the form:

For binary operations, the syntax is in the form:

For tertiary operations, the syntax is in the form:

Many of the operators are made up of two symbols combined together. This is necessary because of a lack of enough distinct symbols on the keyboard. Whenever you have such an operator e.g. >=, you cannot write it as > =. (Notice the included space).

WinRunner supports six different types of operations. These are:

Arithmetic

Arithmetic operations are used for performing calculations. The operands of an arithmetic operation should be numeric values and the result of this operation is numeric. The arithmetic operators available in TSL are shown in Table 11.5:

Operator	Description	Usage Example	
+	Addition	foo = 4 + 2;	# foo has the value 6
-	Subtraction	foo = 4 - 2;	# foo has the value 2
	Negation	foo = -4;	# foo has the value -4
*	Multiplication	foo = 4 * 2;	# foo has the value 8
/	Division	foo = 4 / 2;	# foo has the value 2
%	Modulo	foo = 4 % 2;	# foo has the value 0
^ or **	Exponent	foo = 4 ^ 2;	# foo has the value 16
++	Increment	foo++;	# The value of foo increases by 1

--	Decrement	foo --;	# The value of foo decreases by 1

Table 11.5: Arithmetic operators.

Comparison

Comparison operators are used to compare two values against each other. The two values being compared should be of a similar type e.g. you should compare two number against each other and two strings against each other. The result of a comparison operation is the Boolean value of 1 (for true) or 0 (for false). Table 11.6 shows the comparison operators available in TSL.

Operator	Description	Usage Example	
==	Equality	4 == 2	# the result is 0 (false)
!=	Inequality	4 != 2	# the result is 1 (true)
>	Greater than	4 > 2	# the result is 1 (true)
<	Less than	4 < 2	# the result is 0 (false)
>=	Greater than or equals	4 >= 2	# the result is 1 (true)
<=	Less than or equals	4 <= 2	# the result is 0 (false)

Table 11.6: Comparison operators.

Logical

Logical operators exist to allow us to reduce the value of several Boolean operations to a single Boolean answer. The results of Boolean operations can be combined in three ways:

Conjunctions: when both operands in the logical operation are necessary for a condition to be satisfied.

Disjunctions: when only one operand of the logical operation is needed to satisfy a condition.

Negation: When the value of an operand is reversed.

Table 11.7 provides the list of logical operators available in TSL.

Operator	Description	Usage Example	
&&	And (Conjunction)	4 > 2 && 0 > 2	# the result is 0 (false)

| || | Or (Disjunction) | 4 > 2 \|\| 0 > 2 | # the result is 1 (true) |
| ! | Not (Negation) | !(4 > 2) | # the result is 0 (false) |

Table 11.7: Logical operators.

Concatenation

Concatenation allows you to join two values as strings. The ampersand (&) character is used for concatenation. An example of this operation is:

foo = "Hello " & " World";   # foo has the value *Hello World*

Assignment

Assignment statements change the value of a variable. The equal sign (=) is the assignment operator and the operation simply evaluates the expression on the right side of the assignment operator and assigns this value to the storage container on the left side of the assignment operator.

Several shortcut forms also exist for combining an assignment operation with other types of operations. These shortcuts and their expanded forms are listed in Table 11.8 below:

Operator	Usage Example	Comparable construct
+=	foo += 2;	foo = foo + 2;
-=	foo -= 2;	foo = foo – 2;
*=	foo *= 2;	foo = foo * 2;
/=	foo /= 2;	foo = foo / 2;
%=	foo %= 2;	foo = foo % 2;
^= or **=	foo ^= 2; foo **= 2;	foo = foo ^ 2; foo = foo ** 2;
&=	foo &= "Hello";	foo = foo & "Hello";

Table 11.8: Assignment operators.

CAUTION: You must not put a space between symbols when operators are made up of two or more symbols.

Conditional

Conditional operators are used as a shorthand method for performing assignments based on the result of a condition. The ? and : operators are involved in this operation and they are used in the following syntactic form:

In this construct, if the condition evaluates to true, the variable is set to the value of the expression indicated by truevalue. However, if the condition is false, the variable is set to falsevalue.

Branching

Branching statements allow your code to avoid executing certain portions of code unless a specified condition is met. This condition must resolve to a Boolean value of true or false. When the condition evaluates to true, we say that the condition is met and when it evaluates to false, we say the condition is not met.

TSL uses the resulting value of a condition to decide what code to execute. There are two forms of branching statements supported in TSL and these are the if statement and the switch statement.

NOTE: In TSL, 1 represents a Boolean value of true, and 0 represents a Boolean value of false.

If Statements

The first form of a branching statement that we will look at is the if statement. This statement allows users to execute code only if a certain condition is met. The syntax for the if statement is shown above, but though it looks intimidating, it isn't. The syntax represents the three different forms of writing the if statement. These forms are:

The if Form

113

In this form of the if statement, the specified statements are only executed if the condition evaluates to true. If the condition is false then no associated statements are executed. An example of this is:

```
if ( x > 0 ) {
  pause("Positive");
}
```

This displays the message "Positive" in a dialog when the value of *x* exceeds 0 and does nothing otherwise. This is the simplest form of the if statement.

The if-else Form

In this form, one of the two sets of statement will always be executed. If the specified condition evaluates to true, the statements in the if block are executed. However, if the condition evaluates to false, then the elsestatements are executed.

Since the condition can never be both true and false at the same time, only one set of statements are executed. Therefore, this form is best suited for an either-or situation where you always expect to either execute *statements a* or *statements b*. The following code displays an example of using this form of the if statement:

```
if ( x > 0 ) {
  pause("Positive");
} else {
  pause("Not positive");
}
```

When this TSL code block executes, the message "Positive" is displayed when the value is greater than zero, if the value is zero or less, then the message "Not Positive" is displayed. In all instances, you will always see one message or the other.

The if-else-if Form

This form is best suited for a multiple-choice scenario where you want to execute a single set of statements based on a list of conditions. Notice that there are multiple conditions and the adjacent code is only executed if the entry condition is met. The following code is an example of this form:

```
if ( foo > 0 ) {
  pause("Positive");
}
else if ( foo == 0 ) {
  pause("Zero");
}
else {
  pause("Negative");
}
```

When this executes, only one set of TSL code is executed. The evaluation of the conditions begins from the first line and once a condition evaluates to true, the related code block is executed. From my example, you may notice that at any time, a value can only be greater than zero, zero, or less than zero.

You should be careful to ensure that two conditions cannot evaluate to true at the same time, if they do, only the first scenario where the condition evaluates to true is executed as shown in the following code:

```
if ( foo > 0 ) {
  pause("Positive");
}
else if ( foo > 20 ) {
  pause("Greater than 20");
}
else if ( foo == 0 ) {
  pause("Zero");
}
else {
  pause("Negative");
}
```

when foo > 20 is true, foo > 0 is also true. But because foo > 0 is evaluated before foo > 20 (due to its location in the if statement) the message "Greater than 20" can never be seen. You should be careful to avoid this in your code.

switch statement

Another branching statement that is supported in TSL is the switch statement. The switch statement uses the value of a single controlling expression to determine the appropriate set of statements to execute. As shown above, the switch statement contains a list of constant values and whichever matches the testexpression determines the set of code to execute.

The execution of a switch statement can be described to run in the following order:

1. The testexpression is evaluated.

2. Each case statement within the switch statement is evaluated and if the constant value matches the value of the testexpression, the embedded statements are executed.

3. If no case statement has a matching value, the embedded statements in the default label are executed.

4. If no case statement has a matching value and there is no default label, no code is executed in the switch statement and execution continues with the next statement after the switch statement.

The following code uses a switch statement to evaluate an input variable and determines if the variable matches Y or N.

```
switch (foo)
{
    case "Y", "y":
        pause("Yes");
        break;
    case "N", "n":
        pause("No");
        break;
    default:
        pause("Unkown value");
}
```

Notice that the case statement has both "Y" and "y" because we wish to do a case insensitive comparison. You may also notice the break statement that is included after each case statement. This is used to prevent run through, if you don't use the break statement, the code from your case label and the following case label will be executed.

Loops

Loops provide the ability to repeat execution of certain statements. These statements are repeatedly executed until an initial condition evaluates to false. TSL supports four different types of loops and these are the while, do..while, for and for..in loops.

We will now look closely at each of these types of loops, but before we do, we will examine the concept of infinite loops.

Infinite Loops

Due to the fact that a loop repeats the execution of a statement, it is possible for the loop to keep running without stopping. This is known as an infinite loop and it is one of the biggest problems that can occur with loops. It occurs when the condition that shuts off the loop never evaluates to false and thus the loop runs forever. To prevent infinite loops, ensure that:

a. You are modifying the loop variable.

b. The loop condition is written in such a way that will eventually evaluate to false.

We will now look at each of the available loops.

The while Loop

The while loop is the simplest form of the loop and it simply repeats execution until the condition evaluates to false. The following code shows an example of using the while loop.

```
foo = 1;
while ( foo <= 3 ) {
  pause(foo);
  foo++;
}
```

This code displays the numbers 1, 2 and 3 in a message box on execution. Notice that the loop variable is being incremented using the ++ (increment) operator.

The do..while Loop

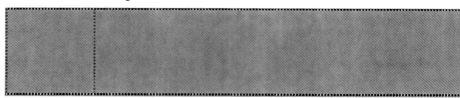

A second form of looping statements is the do..while loop. This loop is used when at least one execution iteration is required of the loop. Notice that the condition is located at the bottom of the loop statement so, all statements embedded within the loop have already been executed at least once. The loop simply allows us to determine whether to repeat execution of the loop.

The following example shows how to use a loop to perform the same operation as the while loop above.

```
foo = 1;
do
{
  pause(foo);
  foo++;
} while ( foo <= 3 );
```

This code displays the values 1, 2, and 3 just as you may expect. Now look at this following example:

```
foo = 10;
do
{
  pause(foo);
  foo++;
} while ( foo <= 3 );
```

In this example, even though the loop variable begins at 10, the loop still executes and displays 10. This is message is only displayed once because in order to continue, the condition must be evaluated and the condition foo <= 3 evaluates to false.

A good way to look at the do..while loop is that it works exactly like a while loop unless in cases when the loop condition initially evaluates to false. In these instances, the while loop will not run at all but the do..while loop will run once.

The for Loop

One of the main criticisms of the other forms of loops is that it is often difficult to track the starting value and loop modification statements. This is because the starting value can occur anywhere before the while or do..while statement, and the loop modification can occur anywhere within the while and do..while statement. This can potentially cause errors where you modify your loop variable twice, or possibly not at all.

The for loop avoids both these problems, as shown about, in the definition statement of the loop, the initializer, condition and modifiers are displayed on the same line. This makes it easy to see what value your loop starts from, the condition that ends the loop and how the loop variable is modified after every iteration.

To be clear, the for loop is very similar in nature to the while loop with the only difference being that it enforces a loop management structure that the while loop lacks. The following code, shows how to use a for loop to rewrite the code we created for our while loop earlier.

```
for ( foo=1; foo <= 3; foo++ ) {
  pause(foo);
}
```

Notice that information about the loop is much easier to read in this structure. Whenever using the for loop, make sure you do not modify the loop variable within the body of the loop. This mistake is easy to make if you are used to working with the while loop.

The for..in loop

The final loop statement which we will look at is the for..in statement. This loop differs from the 3 previous loops we have looked at because it is used to iterate over the values that exist within an array and not until a condition becomes false.

As shown from the syntax, the for..in loop repeats for each value within the array and with each execution, the variable is set to a value within the array. To recreate the same operations we have used for the other loops, we would need the following code:

```
bar = {1, 2, 3};
for ( foo in bar ) {
    pause(foo);
}
```

These are the different loops that exist in TSL. You will agree that the difference between each one of them is mostly subtle. In most cases, each loop form can be used in place of the other so, the type of loop you choose to write is mostly based on what you are most comfortable with.

Loop Modification

When repeating certain operations, there may be instance when you wish to (a) skip execution for the current iteration or (b) stop the loop before the loop condition evaluate to true. TSL provides keywords that can be used to handle these scenarios.

Skipping a loop iteration

When you want to avoid execution for certain values in your loop, you use the continue statement. This statement simply transfers execution to the next iteration of the loop.

```
foo = 1;
while ( foo < 10 ) {
    print( foo++ );
    if ( foo % 2 == 0 ) continue;
}
```

When the above code executes, the values 1, 3, 5, 7 & 9 are printed. For each even number, the condition foo % 2 ==0 evaluates to true and so the continue statement is executed. This skips the loop to the next execution.

Escaping from a Loop

Sometimes in the midst of repeating an activity, you may wish to escape from the loop. For this, you will use the break statement which allows you to exit immediately out of the loop and restart program execution on the next line after the loop.

```
foo = 1;
while ( foo < 10 ) {
    print( foo++ );
    if ( foo % 2 == 0 ) break;
```

```
}
```

On execution, the code prints the values 1 and then escapes from the loop because the foo % 2 == 0 condition evaluates to true.

Functions

Functions are blocks of code containing one or more TSL statements. These code blocks are very useful in performing activities that need to be executed from several different locations in your code. TSL provides many built in functions as well as provides you the ability to create your own user-defined functions.

In TSL, as in most languages, you have the ability to pass information into a function. The function can then process this information. A function also has the ability to return some result from its processing.

There are two steps involved with working with a function. The first step involves creating the function by declaring it. The statements that a function will perform is added in this step and any return values that will be provided is also added at this time. The next step after a function is declared is to call the function. The function call executes the contents of the previously declared function.

We will begin by looking at the two types of functions and then look at the process involved with defining the functions.

Built-In Functions

TSL provides a few hundred functions for various uses. While this may sound daunting, thankfully these functions are broken down into groups. Table 11.9 shows the different groups of built-in functions available in TSL. Also, it is important to remember that certain functions may only be available whenever a specific add-in is included within the environment.

You may refer to Chapter 4 on how to include an add-in.

Function Type	Description
Analog	Functions that are used to track mouse motion over the screen as well as record the clicks of the mouse including the buttons that are clicked. These functions can also be used to track keyboard input.
Context Sensitive	Functions for handling the various GUI objects that exist within the AUT. These functions are inserted by WinRunner into the test as you perform a matching operation in the AUT.
Customization	Functions that allow you to extend the functionality of WinRunner. Using these functions, you can enhance

WinRunner in any of the following ways.

- Add functions to the Function Generator
- Specify new functions to be used in your test during recording
- Create functions for interacting with the user interface
- Create new GUI checkpoints

Standard	Functions for performing several operations such as mathematical computation, string manipulation, date/time interactions, array handling etc.

Table 11.9: Function Types in TSL.

User Defined Functions

When no built in function provides the functionality you want, you may need to create a user-defined function. User-defined functions are different from built-in functions only because you have to define the functions yourself (hence the name user-defined). I'll show you how to define your functions, and then discuss how to invoke both user-defined and built-in functions.

Defining Functions

The syntax structure above shows the structural elements for defining a function. Below, I have provided a detailed description of each item from a function's definition.

class: [optional] Valid values are either static or public. Using public makes the function available to other tests, and in contrast, using static limits access to only the current test or module that defines the function.

functionname: [required] A value conforming to the rules specified in the Naming Rules section defined earlier.

mode: [optional] A value determining the direction of information flow into and out of the function. Each parameter in the parameterlist has a different mode and the valid choices are:

- in – passes a value into the function.
- out – passes a value out of the function.

122

- inout – passes a value into and out of the function.

parameterlist: [required when a mode is specified] A list of comma separated variables that can be used to pass value into a function and also retrieve values from the function. The mode determines whether the variable is used to pass values into or retrieve values from the function.

Functions can also contain a return statement. The return statement may be used to return a value from the function or to terminate execution of the function. The return statement is optional

---

NOTE: All variables used in a function must be declared as either the static or auto class.

```
1     function sum(in var1, inout var2, out var3) {
2         auto answer;
3         answer = var1 + var2;
4         var3 = time_str();
5         return answer;
7     }
```

Listing 11.1: A TSL function definition.

Invoking Functions

To use a function, the function must be invoked. This is also known as calling a function. The process for calling a built-in function is exactly the same as calling a user-defined function. Before you can call any function, you must know the following details:

Purpose: What the function does.

Function Name: The name of the function.

Parameter List: The list of values to pass into the function. This list is comma separated and should match the number of parameters in the function definition. The mode of each of parameter is also important in determining whether to pass a value or variable to a function. I have listed below what you can pass for each mode.

- in – pass a value or a variable.
- out – pass a variable.

- inout – pass a variable.

Return Value: Any value that may be returned from the function. Some functions do not return a value and when they do, you may choose to ignore the return value.

In the code shown in Listing 11.2, I have shown how to invoke the function that was previously defined in Listing 11.1

```
1    static numVar, numResult, strExecution;
2    numVar = 20;
3    numResult = sum( 3, numVar, strExecution);
4    print("Result: " & numResult);
5    print("Execution Date/Time: " & strExecution);
```

Listing 11.2: TSL code to invoke a function.

On execution, this code will display the following in message log window:

```
Result: 23
Execution Date/Time: Thu Apr 26 13:38:41 2007
```

The following describes what happens in each the line of code from Listing 11.2.

Line 1 creates three variables that we will use in this test. Don't forget that variable declaration is optional in TSL.

Line 2 initializes the numVar variable to the value 2.

Line 3 invokes the sum() function. We pass the value 3 to the first parameter of sum() which has a mode of in. The second parameter has an inout mode so we must pass a variable. We pass the value 20 through the variable numVar. The third parameter is mode out so we pass a variable strExecution to this parameter. The value of this variable will be changed in the sum() function. The result of the function call is assigned to our numResult variable.

Line 4 prints out the contents of numResult. This is the sum of the first 2 parameters.

Line 5 prints out the contents of strExecution. This is the date/time when the function was called.

Useful TSL Function

I have included below some very useful TSL functions. These functions have such repeated usage in test creation that it is beneficial to know them by heart. They are:

call – Executes a WinRunner test.

call_ex – Launches QuickTest Professional and executes a QTP test. QTP must be installed on the machine for this function call to work.

file_compare – Compares the contents of two files and writes the result of this comparison to the test results log.

GUI_load – Dynamically loads a GUI Map file into memory and the GUI Map editor. The contents of the GUI Map file can then be used during test execution.

invoke_application – Used to launch an application. This is the preferred way of launching an application instead of navigating through the Windows program menu.

load – Loads a WinRunner function library into memory for usage.

pause – Displays a message in a dialog and pauses test execution until the user dismisses the dialog.

print – Writes out values to the print log. This is useful when you don't want to pause execution, and also don't need the message saved to the test results window.

report_msg – Used to send information to the test result window. This does not affect the result of the test.

set_window – Sets the context window i.e. the window in which all subsequent operations will be performed in. This is perhaps the most imports function in TSL.

tl_step – Marks a step as pass/fail and send the corresponding information to the test result window.

THINGS TO WATCH OUT FOR WHEN WRITING TSL

1. Case sensitivity.

2. Use semi-colon to complete every simple statement.

3. Use curly braces with each compound statement.

4. Pair up double quotes, parentheses and curly braces.

5. Use = for assignment and == for equality.

Summary

In this chapter you have learned about the TSL language. We began by looking at the contents of the language and the different syntax structures that each of the program elements use. Finally, I described the use of functions and provided a list of useful functions that exist in TSL. In the next chapter we will use everything we have learned in created some tests.

CHAPTER 12

PUTTING IT ALL TOGETHER

In this chapter, I will combine all the things we have learnt so far in this book and see how the knowledge can be used in creating tests. The goal of this chapter is to show how to combine all the materials I have presented in the task of creating automated tests. In this chapter, I will reuse the GUI Map file (stored at C:\MyTests\ExpenseCalculator.gui) that we created in Chapter 6.

Test Case: Check Date

Listing 12.1 shows the Check Date test case that ensures that the Expense Calculator application displays the current system date when the Today's Date button is clicked.

```
Test Name:
      Check Date

Purpose:
      Check that the correct system date is displayed im
      mm/dd/yyyy format when the Today's date button is
      clicked.

Pre-Conditon:
      AUT is closed.
```

Step	User Action	Expected Result
1	Launch the AUT	Main application window is displayed
2	Click the Today's	Correct system date in

	Date button	mm/dd/yyyy format is displayed in appropriate textbox.
3	Close the AUT	

```
Post-Condition:
     AUT is closed.

Valid Test Data:
     N/A
```

Listing 12.1: Check Date Test Case.

Solution

1. Create a new test and open the GUI Map file.

The script will hold the recorded TSL statements and any other test artifacts we include. Click on File ▶ New to create a new test. Then, click on Tools ▶ GUI Map Editor to open the GUI Map Editor. Load the GUI Map file from C:\MyTests\ExpenseCalculator.gui.

2. Make sure the initial condition of the application is met.

In this case, we have to ensure that the AUT is closed.

3. Start recording.

In this step, we instruct WinRunner to start monitoring our actions and convert these into appropriate TSL statements. You can start recording using the toolbar Record button, navigating to Test ▶ Record on the menu, or by pressing F2.

4. Perform the test case steps sequentially.

The steps we need to perform are Steps 1, 2 & 3 from Listing 12.1. As we perform these, WinRunner will generate TSL statements matching each operation. Remember that we are currently in recording mode.

5. Stop recording.

Instruct WinRunner to stop recording your actions. This can be done by using the toolbar Stop button, clicking Test ▶ Stop Recording in the menu or by pressing Ctrl_L + F3.

Listing 12.2 shows the test script that is generated by our application.

```
# Shell_TrayWnd
        set_window ("Shell_TrayWnd", 1);
        button_press ("start");

# Start Menu
        set_window ("Start Menu", 1);
        list_select_item ("SysListView32_0", "Expense Calculator");

# frmExpense
        set_window ("frmExpense", 7);
        button_press ("btnDate");
        menu_select_item ("mnuFile;mnuExit");
```

Listing 12.2: Check Date test.

6. Run the test in Debug Mode.

Select Debug Run Mode from the toolbar and invoke the test for execution. This allows us to determine if the recorded test executes properly. From the test result Window, we are only interested in checking whether the test ran to completion without errors.

TIP Make sure the Run in Batch Mode option is not selected in your General Options dialog so that all errors will be displayed during execution.

---

7. Enhance the test with comments.

This is an optional step but it makes it easier for us to know where to edit new details into our test. After including these comments into the test, the test case looks like the content in Listing 12.3.

```
###################################################################
# STEP 1: Launch the AUT
###################################################################
# Shell_TrayWnd
        set_window ("Shell_TrayWnd", 1);
        button_press ("start");

# Start Menu
        set_window ("Start Menu", 1);
        list_select_item ("SysListView32_0", "Expense Calculator");


###################################################################
# STEP 1: Expected Result
```

```
#############################################################

#############################################################
# STEP 2: Click the Today's Date button
#############################################################
# frmExpense
        set_window ("frmExpense", 7);
        button_press ("btnDate");


#############################################################
# STEP 2: Expected result
#############################################################


#############################################################
# STEP 3: Close the AUT
#############################################################
        menu_select_item ("mnuFile;mnuExit");


#############################################################
# STEP 3: Expected result
#############################################################
```

Listing 12.3: Check Date test modified to include comments.

8. Enhance the test by including synchronization points, checkpoints, data parameterization and/or TSL statements.

Here the process gets a little more interesting. We're going to determine what test artifacts we need to add from the following:

Synchronization points – There is no timing issue in the recorded script so we do not need to add any of this.

Checkpoint – We have two items to check.

- The first item involves a check whether a window is displayed so we are doing a static check here. We simply need to check if the window is displayed with the expected label.
- The second check is a little more difficult. It is a dynamic check and not a static one. For this test, if we create the expected result as 02/10/2007 the test result will only be valid for today. To make this test able to be run everyday without modification, we will use TSL code which can be used to perform dynamic checks.

Parameterization – There is no need to include this in the test. We have no hard-coded data values in this test.

TSL Code – We will have to use this for the Step 2 check. TSL allows us to read the current system date and compare it to the content of the Date Textbox. Listing 12.4 shows the included TSL. The sections in bold font are the TSL statements that we inserted. Notice that the statements are inserted within the section specified by the test case where we need verification statements.

```
####################################################################
# $info. getMMDDYYYYDate hshittu 12/31/2006               #
# The getMMDDYYYYDate function retrieves the date from the    #
# system and returns it in MMDDYYYY fromat             #
####################################################################
function getMMDDYYYYDate() {
# Declare variables for usage
  auto date;        #For unformatted system date/time
  auto mm;          #For formatted month
  auto dd;          #For formatted day
  auto yyyy;        #For formatted year
  auto month;       #For unformatted 3 letter month
  auto result;      #For the resulting mm/dd/yyyy value

# Assign values to the variable
  date=time_str();
  dd=substr(date, 9, 2);
  yyyy=substr(date, 21);
  month=substr(date, 5, 3);

# Month is a special case.
# Convert from 3-letter Mon form to 2-number mm form
  switch(month){
          case "Jan": mm="01"; break;
          case "Feb": mm="02"; break;
          case "Mar": mm="03"; break;
          case "Apr": mm="04"; break;
          case "May": mm="05"; break;
          case "Jun": mm="06"; break;
          case "Jan": mm="07"; break;
          case "Feb": mm="08"; break;
          case "Mar": mm="09"; break;
          case "Apr": mm="10"; break;
          case "May": mm="11"; break;
          case "Jun": mm="12"; break;
  }

# Concatenate the result into a variable
  result = mm & "/" & dd & "/" & yyyy;
```

```
# Return the result
  return result;
}


############################################################
# STEP 1: Launch the AUT
############################################################
# Shell_TrayWnd
        set_window ("Shell_TrayWnd", 1);
        button_press ("start");

# Start Menu
        set_window ("Start Menu", 1);
        list_select_item ("SysListView32_0", "Expense Calculator");

############################################################
# STEP 1: Expected Result
############################################################
win_check_info("frmExpense","label","Expense Calculator - (Default)",10);

############################################################
# STEP 2: Launch the AUT
############################################################
# frmExpense
        set_window ("frmExpense", 7);
        button_press ("btnDate");

############################################################
# STEP 2: Expected result
############################################################
edit_check_info("txtDate","value", getMMDDYYYYDate());

############################################################
# STEP 3: Close the AUT
############################################################
        menu_select_item ("mnuFile;mnuExit");

############################################################
# STEP 3: Expected result
############################################################
```

Listing 12.4: Check Date enhanced with TSL.

9. Run the test in Verify Mode.

We have completed creating our test and we will now run it in Verify Mode, so that the result will be preserved. You can do this by clicking the Run From The Top button on the toolbar or selecting Test ▶ Run From The Top from the menu.

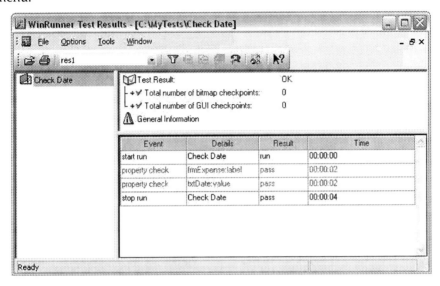

Figure 12.1: Test Result Window for Check Date test.

Figure 12.1 shows the test results for this test. Note that the test passed.

Understanding the test

I have created the getMMDDYYYYDate() function which retrieves the date/time from the system and then reformats it. The time_str() function is used to retrieve the system date/time but this displays it in the following format:

Mon Jan 29 22:02:19 2007

So, the additional code is added to chop up this information into the correct mm/dd/yyyy form and then return this information using the return statement.

Next, within the expected result section of step 2, we use an edit_check_info statement to compare the value of the value property of our txtDate object to the system date in mm/dd/yyyy form. If these two match, the step passes, if not, the step fails.

THE CASE FOR REPEATED TEST EXECUTION

I suggest running your test after making a complete unit of addition e.g. after adding a function, checkpoint, synchronization point etc. The benefit of this repeated execution is that it makes it easy for you to localize the source of error in your test script.

If version x of your test script executes properly, and then you add a test artifact (e.g. a TSL function) and the new version fails because of some syntax error, it will be easy to identify that the error is being caused by the latest addition.

Test Case: Verify Expense Total

We will now work on another test employing the same process we used in the Check Date test. Listing 12.5 shows the Verify Expense Total test case that calculates the amount of expenses shown in the grid and ensures that they add up to the amount in the total's textbox.

```
Test Name:
        Verify Expense Total

Purpose:
        Ensure that the contents of the Amount column add up to
        the amount shown in the total's textbox. The amount in
        the textbox should be formatted in $#,###.00 format.

Pre-Conditon:
        AUT is closed. The total amount in the open account
        exceeds $1,000.00
```

Step	User Action	Expected Result
1	Launch the AUT	Contents of the Amount column add up to the amount shown in the Total's textbox. The totals should be displayed in $#,###.00 format.
2	Close the AUT	

```
Post-Condition:
        AUT is closed.

Valid Test Data:
        N/A
```

Listing 12.5: Verify Expense Total Test Case.

Solution

1. Create a new test and open the GUI Map file.

Don't forget to load the GUI Map file.

2. Make sure the initial condition of the application is met.

3. Start recording.

4. Perform the test case steps sequentially.

5. Stop recording.

Listing 12.6 shows the test script that is generated from our recording session.

```
# Shell_TrayWnd
        set_window ("Shell_TrayWnd", 1);
        button_press ("start");

# Start Menu
        set_window ("Start Menu", 1);
        list_select_item ("SysListView32_0", "Expense Calculator");

# frmExpense
        set_window ("frmExpense", 7);
        menu_select_item ("mnuFile;mnuExit");
```

Listing 12.6: Verify Expense Total test.

6. Run the test in Debug Mode.

Remember to check that the Run in Batch Mode option is not set in the General Options dialog.

7. Enhance the test with comments.

This optional step makes it easier for us to insert test artifacts. The resulting code is shown in Listing 12.7.

```
############################################################
# STEP 1: Launch the AUT
############################################################
# Shell_TrayWnd
        set_window ("Shell_TrayWnd", 1);
        button_press ("start");
```

```
# Start Menu
        set_window ("Start Menu", 1);
        list_select_item ("SysListView32_0", "Expense Calculator");

################################################################
# STEP 1: Expected Result
################################################################

################################################################
# STEP 2: Close the AUT
################################################################
# frmExpense
        set_window ("frmExpense", 7);
        menu_select_item ("mnuFile;mnuExit");
################################################################
# STEP 2: Expected result
################################################################
```

Listing 12.7: Verify Expense Totals test modified to include comments.

8. Enhance the test by including synchronization points, checkpoints, data parameterization and/or TSL statements.

This is the most challenging part of the test so far. We're going to determine what test artifacts we need to add from the following:

Synchronization points – None needed.

Checkpoint – We have one item to check.

- The check compares the contents of the totals textbox to the summation of amounts from the grid. I will use a simple GUI check to compare the value of the totals textbox to the computed value.

Parameterization – None needed.

TSL Code – We will have to use TSL for the check above. TSL allows us to loop through the contents of the grid and sum the values. The GUI checkpoint will then compare the value in the total's textbox to this value. Listing 12.8 shows the inserted TSL statements.

```
################################################################
# $info. getTotalAmount hshittu 12/31/2006              #
# The getTotalAmount function sums the contents of the Amount  #
# column in the grid                                    #
################################################################
function getTotalAmount(){
# Declare variables for usage
```

136

```
  auto numRows;
  auto numCounter;
  auto numResult;
  auto numAmount;

# Assign values to the variable
  set_window("frmExpense", 1);
  ActiveX_get_info("acxExpenses","Rows", numRows);

  numResult = 0;
  for (numCounter=1; numCounter<numRows; numCounter++) {
    ActiveX_set_info("acxExpenses","Row", numCounter);
    ActiveX_set_info("acxExpenses","Col", 5);
    ActiveX_get_info("acxExpenses","Text", numAmount);
          numResult = numResult + numAmount;
  }

# Return the result
  return numResult;
}

##################################################################
# $info. getTotalAmount hshittu 12/31/2006                       #
# The getTotalAmount function sums the contents of the Amount    #
# column in the grid                                             #
##################################################################
function formatNumbers(in numData){
  auto parts[];              #Holds the whole & decimal parts of the number
  auto strDecimal;           #Holds the decimal part of the input
  auto strWhole;             #Holds the whole part of the input
  auto strFormat;            #Holds the formatted whole & decimal parts of the number
  auto numLoop;              #Loops variable for formatting the a value
  auto numStart;             #Index within the input string to start formatting

  split(numData, parts, ".");
  strWhole = parts[1];
  strDecimal = parts[2];

  numStart = length(strWhole) % 3;
  strFormat = substr(strWhole, 1, numStart);
  for (numLoop=numStart+1; numLoop <= length(strWhole); numLoop=numLoop+3) {
    if (strFormat == "") {
      strFormat = substr(strWhole, numLoop, 3);
    } else {
      strFormat = strFormat & "," & substr(strWhole, numLoop, 3);
    }
  }
```

```
#Pad the decimal values with zeros
 if (length(strDecimal) == 0) {
  strDecimal = strDecimal & "00";
 } else if (length(strDecimal) == 1) {
  strDecimal = strDecimal & "0";
 }

# Return the result
 return  "$" & strFormat & "." & strDecimal;
}
```

```
static strExpectedTotal;        #This will hold the expected total
```

```
################################################################
# STEP 1: Launch the AUT
################################################################
# Shell_TrayWnd
        set_window ("Shell_TrayWnd", 1);
        button_press ("start");

# Start Menu
        set_window ("Start Menu", 1);
        list_select_item ("SysListView32_0", "Expense Calculator");
```

```
################################################################
# STEP 1: Expected Result
################################################################
# frmExpense
set_window("frmExpense", 1);
strExpectedTotal = formatNumbers(getTotalAmount());
edit_check_info("txtTotal","value",strExpectedTotal);
```

```
################################################################
# STEP 2: Close the AUT
################################################################
        menu_select_item ("mnuFile;mnuExit");
```

```
################################################################
# STEP 2: Expected result
################################################################
```

Listing 12.8: Verify Expense Totals enhanced with TSL.

9. Run the test in Verify Mode.

We have completed creating our test and we will now run it in Verify Mode, so that the result will be preserved.

Understanding the test

I have created the getTotalAmount() function that sums all the values in the Amount column of the grid. I have also created the formatCurrency() function with accepts a number as input and returns the number in $#,###.00 format.

Next, within the expected result section of step 1, we use an edit_check_info statement to compare the value of the value property of our txtTotal object to the value returned by the formatCurrency function. If these two match, the step passes, if not, the step fails.

Summary

In this chapter we have looked at 2 tests that have allowed us to practice the different concepts we have learned so far. I strongly suggest returning to this chapter after you have completed this book until you are sure you have a complete understanding of what has been discussed here.

CHAPTER 13

RUNNING & DEBUGGING TESTS

After we have completed this test, we are now ready to run the recorded test. For this first test execution, we will run the test in debug mode simply to verify that the test is correct. If we discover that the test has errors, we will need to use the debugging tools provided by WinRunner to help identify the problem.

CAUTION: At this time, we are checking for errors in the test and not in the AUT. Errors in the AUT are defects and are fixed by developers.

Only after we know the test is correct do we begin to run the test in verify mode. In this chapter, I will discuss how to run the test as well as how to debug the test.

Running The Test

I have mentioned all three modes of test execution previously. In this chapter, we will look at these modes and when it is best to use each one. Additionally WinRunner provides many ways in which a test can be executed. I will describe each of these also.

Test Run Modes

A run mode determines how WinRunner runs the test after the test is executed. Run modes can be chosen from the Test toolbar and must be specified before you start executing the test.

The three modes available are:

Update Run Mode – This mode is used to update the expected results of checkpoints. Whenever WinRunner executes a test in this mode, it updates the expected results folder with values it recorded during program execution. You should be careful about running a test in this mode. If you mistakenly run a test in this mode, you may need to verify that your expected results still match what s requested in your test case.

Debug Run Mode – This mode is very similar to the Verify Run Mode with the difference that when tests are executed in this mode, the results folder is overwritten each time. The Debug Run Mode is a useful space saving feature.

Verify Run Mode – This mode is used to execute tests after they have been certified as error-free. Whenever a test is executed in this mode, a new results folder is generated to store the test results. WinRunner preserves all results of test execution whenever this mode is used.

You can choose to overwrite a previous test result by simply specifying an existing run name. Figure 13.1 shows that dialog that you are presented with once you launch a test in Verify Run Mode.

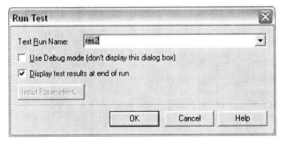

Figure 13.1: The Run Test dialog.

You may notice that using this dialog you can switch the test run mode to debug mode simply by clicking the Use Debug mode checkbox. To run this test in update mode, you will have to click the cancel button and choose the Update Run Mode from the Test toolbar.

Now that you have selected the mode you want the test to run in, we will now talk about the commands to use in running the test. I will also provide the commands that can be used to pause and stop the test execution.

The following commands are used to launch the test:

Run from Top – This command executes the test starting from the first line of executable TSL code in the test.

Run from Arrow – Starts test execution from the line of script marked with the execution arrow. You can specify the starting point for this type of execution by right clicking in the left margin of the test window. This marks the line you clicked on with the execution arrow. This command is useful for continuing test execution after pausing.

Run Minimized – Allows you to launch the test from the first statement o from the execution arrow. Using this command, the WinRunne window is minimized when test execution begins and restored whei the test execution completes. This allows the entire screen to be available to the AUT.

To stop a test at any time during execution, you can use the Stop toolbar button from the Test toolbar or click on Test ▶ Stop Test Run.

PAUSING A TEST

WinRunner provides a few mechanisms for ending your test execution. These include:

Clicking the Pause button during test execution. The effect of this is that the test is paused and can be restarted from the beginning using Test ▶ Run from the Top or continued from the current location using Test ▶ Run from Arrow.

Using the pause() TSL function to pause the script. This function displays some provided information in a message box and gives you the option of click on **Pause** or **Continue**. Execution is suspended until a user chooses either of these options.

Using a breakpoint - I have described this earlier in the chapter.

Debugging The Test

debug (dē-bŭg)

verb.

1. to detect and remove defects or errors from.
2. *Computer Science:* to detect and remove errors from (a computer program).

You would have realized by now that the TSL script you create doesn't always do what you intended for it to do. You may have incorrectly recorded your test case or entered some faulty TSL code. Whatever the case may be, whenever there are errors in your test script, you have to fix them before you can start analyzing the test results. It is this systematic process of removing bugs from our test script that is known as debugging.

There are 2 types of errors that can exist in a test script. These are:

- Syntactic: An error involving TSL syntax.

- Semantic: An error in the logic of the test script.

Syntax error are often far easier to find because once the TSL interpreter helps identify the problem. Whenever the interpreter comes across these errors, it highlights the erroneous statements and indicates that it doesn't understand the command. I suggest looking a few lines above and below the highlighted statement to find the source of the syntax problem. Some of the most common source of syntax problems include:

- Typographical errors in a variable or function name
- Forgetting the case sensitive nature of TSL names
- Missing or improperly placed semicolons

A test with semantic errors may still run without failing, but would often produce incorrect results. To find errors of this type, a more powerful means of tracing through the code is needed. This is known as debugging.

Debugging is a systematic process that requires patience and clear analysis. The tools provided by WinRunner aid you in debugging your code but do not identify what the problem is. They simply make it easier for you to discover the problem. To make this connection, I will use an analogy. If something happens in a movie you are watching, and you want to see it clearly, you will use the remote control to pause the movie and step through the scene frame by frame. Stepping through the scene allows you to inspect the program execution and more clearly see what you wanted. The remote doesn't point out what you have missed, it only allows you to view the scene closely.

This is exactly what happens in debugging. The WinRunner debugging tools allow you to pause test execution and execute your code step-by-step. After each step of execution, you may use any of the available tools to observe the following information:

- Value of variables and expressions.
- State of the data table.
- Application execution call chain.

A debugging session can be performed using the following steps

1. Choose debug mode for the test execution.

In this mode, we will overwrite the test results each time we run the test. This is acceptable because we are checking to see whether the test has errors. As discussed earlier, this mode saves disk space.

2. Run the test to identify the problem.

Obviously if there are no errors noted, you will not need to debug. However, if an error occurs during execution, you will need to debug the test. If several problems exist, note them down and only tackle one at a time. Often, fixing one problem may impact the existence of another.

3. Set up a break point.

Identify the problem you want to tackle and set up a breakpoint close to the execution of that line. Choosing the correct breakpoint location is an art and you may have to run the test several times before identifying the ideal breakpoint location. This location should be anywhere before the line where the problem is noted. Of course you can set up a breakpoint at the first line of test execution but this will waste your time if you have to step through the entire test before you get to the problem's location.

Breakpoints allow us to pause test execution whenever the test runs a specific line of TSL code. Using a breakpoint is a far better way to pause the test execution than trying to invoke the pause feature (using Debug ▶ Pause Test Run) when the test is running. A breakpoint can be visually identified by a marker in the left margin of the test window. Figure 13.2 shows the Check Date test with an included breakpoint.

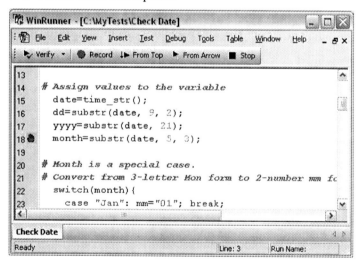

Figure 13.2: A test showing the breakpoint icon in the left margin.

There are two types of breakpoints that can be created in WinRunner. These include:

144

Break at Location - Allows you to pause the test when it reaches a specific line of execution. This breakpoint can be added by putting your cursor on the line where you want to create the breakpoint and doing any of the following:

    a.   Clicking the left margin of the test window.
    b.   Menu: Selecting Debug ▶ Toggle Breakpoint.
    c.   New Breakpoint dialog: Selecting Debug ▶ Break in Function.
    d.   Keyboard Shortcut: Press F9.

Break in Function - Allows you to pause test execution when the specified function is invoked. To invoke this breakpoint, the function has to be loaded in memory and then added using the New Breakpoint dialog by selecting Debug ▶ Break in Function.

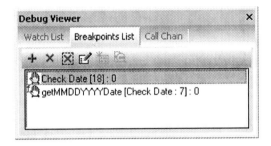

Figure 13.3: The Breakpoint List pane.

Figure 13.3 shows the Breakpoints List pane of the Debug Viewer with both a location and function breakpoints. The location breakpoint is in the following format:

Test file [Line]: Pass Count

While the function breakpoint is in the following format:

Function [Test file: Line]: Pass Count

The pass count is the number of times the breakpoint should be skipped before being triggered.

TIP: You can delete a breakpoint by using the delete icon from the Breakpoint list pane of the Debug Viewer.

---

4. Step through the code.

Once you have set up your breakpoints, run the code and wait for the execution to reach the breakpoint statement. When the code reaches the breakpoint you have defined, it will pause. You can tell that the code is paused when the execution arrow overlays the breakpoint icon in the left margin of the test window.

NOTE: The execution arrow is a yellow arrow displayed in the left margin that signifies the next statement to be executed.

Now, we will step through our code execution. This means running the application one line at a time. There are 4 different ways in which you can step through code and these are:

Step - This executes the current line of TSL code. If the line of code to be executed is a user-defined test, or an invocation of another test, the entire called item is executed in a single step.

Step Into - This executes the current line of TSL code unless the line of code to be executed is a user-defined test, or an invocation of another test. In this case, the command enters into the called function/test.

Step Out - This executes the current line of TSL code unless the line of code to be executed is within a user-defined test, or an invoked test. In this case, the command completes the rest of the statements in the function/test and returns to the calling test.

Step to Cursor - This executes all the TSL statements between the execution arrow and your cursor. You can use this to quickly execute several lines of code such as loops, etc.

Table 13.1 provides a side-by-side comparison of three step commands. I have not included the Step to Cursor command in this comparison because you determine how the Step to Cursor command executes based on where you place your cursor.

Operation	Step	Step Into	Step Out
TSL statement	Executes	Executes	Executes
Built-in functions [except call()]	Executes	Executes	Executes
call() function	Executes	Enters	Executes

User-defined function	Executes	Enters	Exits
Invoked tests	Executes	Executes	Exits

Table 13.1: Comparison of step operations.

5. Inspect the variables and expressions.

Anytime you step through a line of code, the value of an item in your test script may change. What you are watching for is when a variable, or expression is provided with an incorrect value.

To find this information, we define a watch. A watch allows you to monitor the value of variables and expressions. Several variables and expressions can be watched at the same time and they constitute a watch list. The entire list of expressions being monitored is available in the Watch List tool.

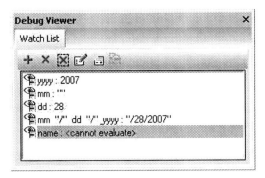

Figure 13.4: The Watch List tool.

Figure 13.4 shows the list of monitored expressions. Notice that the current values of each of these expressions are displayed in the tool. This is the value of the expression based on the current state of execution. As shown in the dialog, both variables and expressions are valid watch items. When a variable is out of scope, the value <cannot evaluate> is provided.

Don't forget that the yellow arrow in the margin denotes the current step about to be executed.

Managing the Watch List

To add an expression to the watch list, click on Debug ▶ Add Watch. The dialog shown in Figure 13.5 is provided. Enter the expression you want to monitor. If you simply want to evaluate the expression without adding it to the watch list, click on Evaluate. To add the expression to the watch list, click on Ok.

147

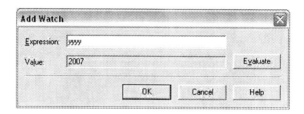

Figure 13.5: Expression dialog.

The Watch List dialog toolbar provides some useful features that can be used in managing each entry in the watch list. To manage any of the items in the watch list, simply highlight the Watch List expression and click the relevant toolbar item in the Watch List.

6. Make necessary code changes.

Based on the values of the inspected expressions, you should now have the ability to localize any erroneous code that needs to be modified. I must stress that the debugging tool will not tell you what the problem is, but by viewing the variables and expressions you should be able to identify the problems.

7. Repeat.

Any seasoned programmer will tell you that the process of debugging is painstakingly meticulous. After making a change to the test script, you will need to run the code again to see if the error still exists. If it does, you will need to repeat steps 3 through 6. If the first error is fixed, then move on to the next error you have and repeat the process. Note that you may need to add/remove breakpoints and watches.

NOTE: Debugging is an acquired skill, but a useful one. Practice with small TSL test scripts to view the execution chain. Over time, you will find it easy to debug a variety of more complex errors.

Once your test is error-free, you should run your test in Verify Mode. Congratulations, you have completed your test. In the next chapter, we will look at how to analyze your test results.

CALL CHAIN

During code execution, it is common for one function to invoke another function, and this second function call yet another function. This chain of function calls is known as the call chain and when debugging your test, it is sometimes useful to see where your function was invoked from. This information is displayed in the Call Chain pane of the Debug Viewer.

The current function is displayed at the top of the call stack and the function that called that function is displayed below it. So, if function foo() invokes function bar(), you will see this listed in the call chain dialog as:

bar()
foo()

Clicking on any of these items moves the yellow execution arrow in the margin of the test window to the line where the function was called from.

Summary

In this chapter you have learned:

- The different test execution modes and what they do.

- How to run a test, pause a test and stop test execution.

- What debugging is and the process for debugging a test.

CHAPTER 14

ANALYZING RESULTS

After the execution of our test, we need to analyze the test execution result to determine whether the test passed or failed. The tool provided for this process is the WinRunner Test Results tool. We will look closely at the process of using this tool to analyze test results. We will later look at some of the useful features of the tool.

Test Results

Whenever you run a test in WinRunner, the results are stored within a test run folder and the Test Results tool is preloaded with this result. If you run your test in Update Mode or Verify Mode, WinRunner invokes the Test Result Viewer once your test completes. If you run your test in Debug mode however, the viewer does not display automatically. You will have to invoke it by clicking on Tools ▶ Test Results.

The Test Results tool displays detailed information about synchronization points, checkpoints, major events that occurred during test execution, messages displayed during execution etc. The tool is shown in Figure 14.1, we will now look closely at the contents of the test results viewer.

The Test Result tool can easily be separated into 5 parts. These include:

Menu – Containing standard operations that can be performed using this tool.

Toolbar – Containing a subset of commands available within the menu. These commands are the one used most often with the tool

Test Tree – Provides a tree based view of test results that are being viewed. The test tree often contains only a single item unless the call function was used in the test script in which case multiple tests are shown in this tree.

Test Summary – A brief summary of the test selected within the Test Tree pane. This provides a quick way to determine if your test passed or failed as well as details about the test.

Test Log – A detailed description about the test execution. The test log provides a color-coded series of messages about the test execution. For certain test elements such as checkpoints, additional details are provided.

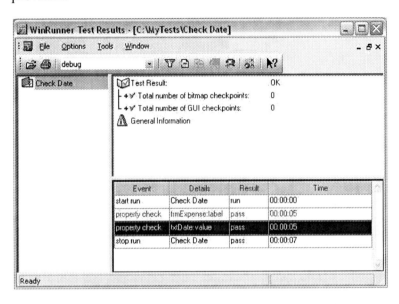

Figure 14.1: The Test Results Viewer.

Some of these parts provide additional details and we will take a closer look at these items.

Test Result Features

The test results tool contains certain features that are useful for result analysis and management. These features include the ability to:

Choose a Test Run – A single test can be executed multiple times with each result preserved under a different run name. Using the toolbar, a specified test run can be selected and the result is displayed.

Filter the results – Especially useful for test results with a large number of events, this feature allows you to limit the type of events that are shown in the test log. Figure 14.2 shows the available filters.

Report the Defect – By using the toolbar icon or clicking on Tools ▶ Report Bug, a predefined connection to Quality Center is used to invoke the Quality Center defect management tool.

Create a Report – By selecting Tools ▶ Text Results, the Windows Notepad tool is invoked and the test result is displayed as a text document. This result can be saved, or printed.

Figure 14.2: Available filters for test results.

Test Summary

Table 14.1 lists the information that can be found within the Test Summary section of the Test result window:

Field	Summary
Test Result	Indicates whether the test passed, failed, or was not completed. For a batch test, this details the result of the batch test and not the individual tests run within the batch test.
Total number of bitmap checkpoints	The total number of bitmap checkpoints executed in the test. Double-clicking on this item can access each of the checkpoints.
Total number of GUI checkpoints	The total number of bitmap checkpoints executed in the test. Each of these checkpoints can also be accessed by double-clicking on this item. Note that a Single Property GUI Checkpoint is not included in this count.

General Information	General detail about the test including the date, operator name, expected results folder and total run time.

Table 14.1: Fields from the Test Summary pane.

Test Log

The test log provides details about the test execution, recording details such as the start and stop of test execution, information about each check point, messages written to the test log, runtime errors and invocations of other tests.
Table 14.2 shows the fields displayed within the Test Log.

Field	Summary
Line	The line number where the event occurred.
Event	The detail that occurred.
Details	Additional information about what happened on the line.
Result	The resulting value of the event, where applicable.
Time	The time during the test execution when the event occurred.

Table 14.2: Fields from the Test Log pane.

In addition to the information from Table 14.2, the test log also uses color-coded identifiers. The following colors are used to display certain information.

Green: Used to display successful events such as checkpoints that pass.

Red: Used to display successful events such as failed checkpoints, system errors etc.

Black: Used to log other messages that do not have a passed/failed status such as messages recorded using the report_msg function, start and stop statements in the test etc.

Double-clicking on certain lines within the test log displays additional information. These lines that generate provide additional details include lines for checkpoint events and file comparisons. We will now look closely at these additional details.

Viewing Checkpoint Details

As I mentioned, when you double-click a line in the test log that represents certain events, WinRunner provides additional details about the event. We will now examine events that contain additional information and examine the extra details that are provided.

Single Property GUI Checkpoint

The simplest checkpoint is the Single Property GUI checkpoint that checks the value of a single object property. This checkpoint can be used to determine whether a specific property has the desired value e.g. whether the focused property of a text field is set to true. For this checkpoint, the additional details from the test log are displayed in a dialog showing the user the expected value and the actual value captured during runtime. Figure 14.3 shows the Property dialog used in presenting this information.

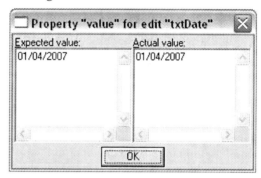

Figure 14.3: Details for a Single Property GUI checkpoint.

If there is a difference in the values, the step is marked as failed.

GUI Checkpoint

For other GUI checkpoints, the test log contains detailed information about the checkpoint using a table format. These checkpoints use a checklist during creation and in the test results log, the same checklist is provided.

Each of the checklist items selected for the checkpoint is included in a table with expected and actual values for each item. An icon is used to distinguish between each of the properties that passed the check and those that failed. Figure 14.4 provides a sample of this details dialog.

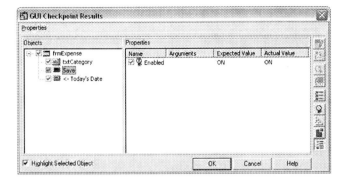

Figure 14.4: Details for a GUI checkpoint.

Test Invocation

When another test is invoked (using a call statement), the event in the test log is the result of the call to the invoked test. To view the complete execution details of the invoked test, double click on the call event line in the event log.

Database Checkpoints

Additional details are similarly provided in a table format with each of the checklist items chosen during the checkpoint creation displayed in a table format. As shown in Figure 14.5, both the expected and actual results are displayed for each checklist item.

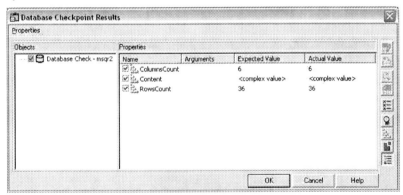

Figure 14.5: Details for a database checkpoint.

Bitmap Checkpoint

The additional details provided for a bitmap checkpoint are a little bit different. Bitmap checkpoints basically compare two images during test execution. When a Bitmap checkpoint fails, it is important to get detailed information about the image mismatch. WinRunner provides this detail by showing three separate dialogs each of them containing an image. The images provided in each of these dialogs are:

Expected result – An image of the result expected.

Actual result – The actual image found by the application.

Difference – An image showing the difference between the actual and expected images. The matching areas are white in the image with the deltas being shown in shades of gray.

Figure 14.6 shows these three dialogs. Notice that in the caption of each of the windows, information about the type of the image being displayed is provided.

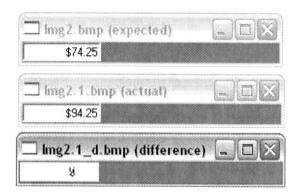

Figure 14.6: The images provided for a bitmap checkpoint.

When a Bitmap checkpoint passes, only one image is provided, because when there is no mismatch, the expected and actual results are identical and there is no difference.

File Comparison

To compare two files, a file_compare TSL function is used. This function compares the contents of both files and writes a message to the test result window whether both files are similar or different. The additional details provided by this event show the actual differences between both files. The complete contents of both files are shown side by side with any lines that differ between the two files highlighted. Figure 14.7 shows the dialog that is provided for a file comparison.

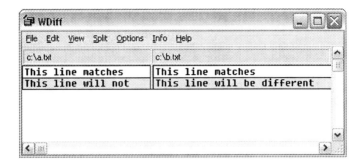

Figure 14.7: Details for a file comparison.

Unified Report View

In addition to the WinRunner Report view, test results can also be viewed in a new reporting tool called the Unified Report view. The Unified Report tool is a standalone application that is installed as a part of the WinRunner installation. This tool can be launched from the Windows program menu by selecting WinRunner ▶ Unified Report. It provides the same results as we have discussed in this chapter but the visual layout is similar to that of a QuickTest Professional test result. Remember that QTP is the other automated testing tool offered by Mercury.

To inform WinRunner to generate test results in the unified report format, select Tools ▶ General Options ▶ Run ▶ Report View and select the Generate unified report information checkbox. If you want to use the Unified Report view as the main test results viewing tool in WinRunner, select the Unified report view option box on the same dialog.

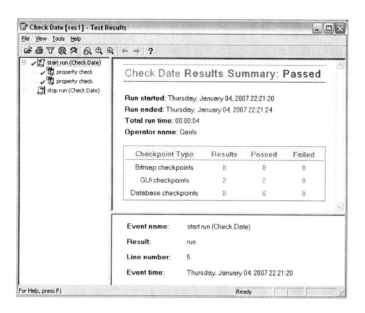

Figure 14.8: Unified Report Tool.

Figure 14.8 shows how this tool looks when displaying the same test result as I have shown in Figure 14.1. Notice that the test result details are similar.

Summary

In this chapter you have learned:

- The different parts of a WinRunner test result

- How to gather useful details from the test result

- Useful features of the Test Results tool

- An alternate Test Result tool that displays data in the format of a QuickTest Professional test result.

CHAPTER 15

BATCH TESTS

batch (bằch)

noun.

3.   a collection of things or persons to be handled together.
4.   *Computer Science:* A set of data or jobs to be processed in a single program run.

Although batch tests might sound like a completely different type of test, they are nothing more than a method of grouping several WinRunner tests to be executed serially. A batch test is created by including several call() statements within a test script. These call() statements are TSL functions and reference an existing test. When the batch test is executed, all the tests that are referenced are invoked. The batch test is therefore said to direct the execution of several other tests.

Without a batch test, if you have 30 tests to run, you will have to run these tests one at a time, waiting for one test to finish before running the next one. While this is certainly possible to do, it is quite tedious. And isn't one of the benefits of an automated testing tool the ability to avoid tedious task?

With a batch test, you simply specify all the tests you want to run in the order that you want to run them. The batch test is invoked with a single run command and the batch test runs until all the referenced tests have been executed. This is the major benefit of a batch test. It provides a tester with the ability to define a long (very long) sequence of tests in a batch test, execute the batch test, leave and then return at a later time to view the results of all the tests that were invoked by the batch test. This frees up a testers time to do other thing. Batch tests are especially suited to run overnight or over a weekend. Figure 15.1 shows how a batch test acting a s a driver, references other existing tests.

159

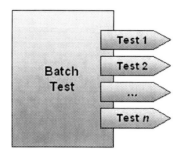

Figure 15.1: Structure diagram of a batch test.

NOTE: Before you create a batch test, you should create all the tests that will be referenced in the batch test.

On execution of a batch test, each test referenced by the batch test is opened from the storage location on the file-system, executed, and the test results are saved within the test results folder of the batch test.

Creating a Batch Test

The process of creating a batch test is similar to creating a regular test. To begin, you must have existing tests you intend to run and know the location of these tests on your filesystem. In this book, I will continue to use the C:\MyTests folder that was created earlier and also use some of the tests we have previously created.

The main function that is used in batch tests is the call() function. This TSL function causes WinRunner to load the referenced test and execute the content of that test. Listing 15.1 shows a simplified form of a batch test.

```
call "c:\\MyTests\\Check Date" ();
call "c:\\MyTests\\Check App Details" ();
call "c:\\MyTests\\Verify Expense Totals" ();
```

Listing 15.1: A simple batch test.

NOTE: Use two \\ here instead of a \. Please refer to Chapter 11 about escape sequences.

---

6. Create a new test

7. Use the call function to reference all tests that will be a part of your test

8. Change the WinRunner options to run your test in batch mode

9. Run your test.

Since a batch test can also include TSL statements, it is possible to include other programming constructs within a batch test. In Listing 15.2, I have provided a batch test that involves the use of a loop to repeat execution of a list of tests.

```
for (i=0; i<=2; i++)
{
    call "c:\\MyTests\\Check Date" ();
    call "c:\\MyTests\\Check App Details" ();
    call "c:\\MyTests\\Verify Expense Totals" ();
}
```

Listing 15.2: A batch test using additional TSL code.

The batch test shown in Listing 15.2 executes each of the 3 referenced tests 3 times. The test results generated from this is shown later in Figure 15.3.

ASK THE EXPERTS

Q: What is the difference between the *call* and the *load* functions?

A: The load function is used to *load* functions from a compiled module into memory, while the *call* function is used to execute a test.

Running a Batch Test

During test execution, dialog windows can be generated by WinRunner to alert the user about errors or to prompt the user to perform an action. While these may be fine for standard tests, they pose a difficulty for batch tests. As I have shown above, a batch test can reference a large number of tests and so take a long time to conclude. Imagine the disappointment if you return to work the next morning to find that your batch test stopped after executing only a few tests because a tester left a pause() statement in their test or had a script error. The loss of time involved with this could be significant.

To solve this problem, batch tests are run in a mode known as batch mode. This mode suppresses all messages that are generated during the tests execution including error messages generated by WinRunner, dialogs displayed using the pause() function etc. so that your test runs without interruption.

To configure WinRunner to run a test in batch mode, I have provided the following steps.

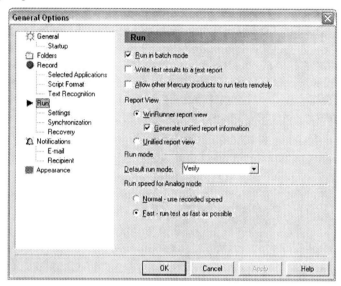

Figure 15.2: The General Options dialog.

QUICKSTEPS: SETTING WINRUNNER TO RUN IN BATCH MODE

1. Open the General Options dialog by clicking Tools ▶ General Options.

2. Select the Run tab.

3. Ensure that the Run in Batch Mode checkbox is checked.

4. Click OK to close the General Options dialog.

Figure 15.2 shows what the dialog looks like after you complete step 3. At the conclusion of all the steps described above, your test is now ready to run in batch mode.

TIP: After executing tests in batch mode, it is recommended that you uncheck the Run in Batch mode option. This way, message dialogs will not be suppressed for other people using the machine.

Batch Test Results

The result of a batch test is a little different from the result of a standard test. For starters, a batch test lists the test results of each of the tests that make up the batch test. It also provides a summary of the result of these tests.

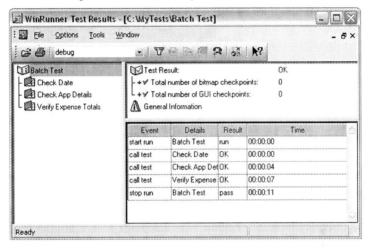

Figure 15.3: Test Result viewer for a batch test.

Figure 15.3 shows the Test Result window of the simple batch test from Listing 15.1. Notice that for each test that you reference, there is a call_test entry listed in the test result log. This represents the execution of the test and you can view the results of this test by double-clicking the call_test entry.

Summary

In this chapter you have learned:

- What batch tests are and the benefits they provide.

- How to create a batch test.

- How to configure WinRunner to run a batch test without and dialogs displayed.

- The contents of a batch test result.

163

CHAPTER 16

RAPIDTEST SCRIPT WIZARD

Sometimes you may want to start your test creation activity with the shortest possible amount of preparation. This may be because you are doing some ad-hoc testing or probably under a deadline to deliver some results. It may also be that you want to quickly complete the process of GUI Map creation. Whatever the case may be, for this jumpstart approach, WinRunner provides a tool that can be used to quickly create a GUI Map and some automated tests. This tool is known as the RapidTest Script Wizard.

The RapidTest Script Wizard is a wizard tool. Similar in nature to some of the wizards I have discussed in this book such as the DataDriver Wizard. Wizards are helper tools that make performing complex tasks easier. A wizard gathers details from you about the operation you want to perform using a series of steps. After gathering all relevant information, the wizard performs the needed operation.

The RapidTest Script Wizard performs exactly like this. It displays a series of pages to the user, with each page asking for some information. Once this information gathering is complete, the wizard creates products based on the answers that were provided.

The WinRunner RapidTest Script Wizard can perform the following tasks:

1. Automatically learn all the objects that exist in an application and save this into a GUI Map file.

2. Create 3 different types of tests.

3. Generate a test template that can be used for future tests.

4. Automatically configure the WinRunner startup to preload certain resources.

Every item that is created by this wizard can be manually created. I have shown you how to do this in the previous chapters. The reason you may want to use the wizard is that it simplifies the test creation process and could be an efficient starting point for working with WinRunner.

Using the RapidTest Script Wizard

The RapidTest Script wizard is available through the Insert menu. You can launch the tool by clicking Insert ▶ RapidTest Script Wizard. Figure 16.1 displays the screen you are presented with on launching the wizard.

NOTE: The RapidTest Script Wizard is not available when certain add-ins are loaded. It is also not available when you are working in GUI Map File per Test mode.

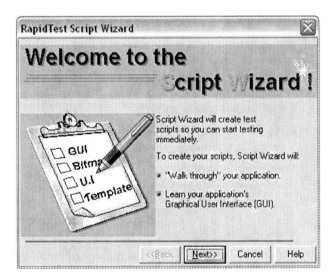

Figure 16.1: Welcome page of the RapidTest Script Wizard.

This first page of the wizard simply welcomes you to the tool and states what functionality the wizard will provide. Click Next and the first interactive screen, shown in Figure 16.2 is displayed.

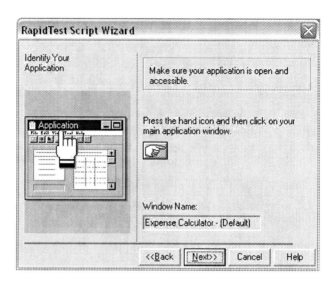

Figure 16.2: The Identify Your Application page.

Using the pointer choose a window in your AUT. The name of this window is immediately displayed in the Window Name field. If you chose the wrong object, simply click on the pointer and try again. Once you have chosen the correct window, click Next.

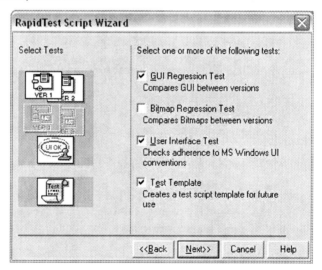

Figure 16.3: The Select Tests page.

The next screen of the wizard is shown in Figure 16.3. In this screen, the wizard prompts you to choose what type of tests it should generate. There are 4 types of tests that can be chosen at this point.

GUI Regression Test: Compares differences in the application GUI between 2 versions of the AUT. This test is used to identify any changes that have been made to objects that exist within the AUT.

Bitmap Regression Test: Similar to a GUI Regression Test, but uses bitmap checkpoints instead. It compares visual differences between two versions of your AUT. Remember that regression tests simply identify differences and that differences are not necessarily defects.

User Interface Test: Tests the conformance of your AUT to specifications provided by Microsoft for application design. While this is a good test to run, remember that for your specific application, the requirements documents determine what is a defect and what isn't.

Test Template: A test script template for use with future tests. It contains TSL code that manages navigation to all the windows in the AUT and can be used as a starting point for any test script.

NOTE: The GUI Regression Test and Bitmap Regression Test are mutually exclusive. This means you can only choose one of the two.

As shown, I have chosen the GUI Regression Test, User Interface Test, and Test Template. Click Next.

TIP: If you are using the wizard simply as a tool to automate the creation of your GUI Map file, you may choose not to select any tests at this step.

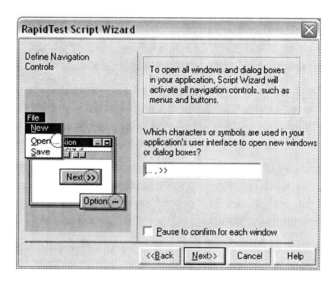

Figure 16.4: The Define Navigation Controls page.

The next step requires you to specify navigational markers that are used to open windows and dialogs in your AUT. By convention, in the Windows environment, programmers use an ellipsis (...) to denote an operation that launches a new window. You may have seen this when you look in the File menu of an application like WinRunner. Additionally, >> is used to specify that a dialog will be opened. As shown in Figure 16.4 even the RapidTest Script Wizard also employs the use of these. (<< is often used to re-open a previously opened dialog so it does not need to be included here).

If your application uses other navigational controls, then you want to include those in this step. For the Expense Calculator application, several menu items launch new dialogs. These include File ▶ New Account, File ▶ Open Account, Actions ▶ View Summary and Help ▶ About. To ensure that the wizard opens all windows, the following values were provided in this field:

..., New Account, Open Account, View Summary

These are the text values on all objects that open a different dialog in Expense Calculator. Notice that the values are separated by commas. Click Next.

168

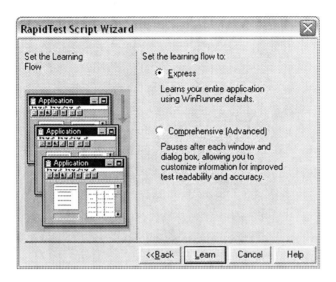

Figure 16.5: The Set the Learning Flow page.

The next dialog requires you to specify the learning flow. The choices are:

Express - WinRunner learns the entire set of objects within your AUT without pausing.

Comprehensive - WinRunner learns all the objects within your AUT and pauses after learning each object to allow you make changes to the recorded properties.

While both choices achieve the same result of creating a GUI Map file, the Comprehensive learning flow provides a greater level of control because it allows you to make changes to the GUI Map file being recorded. Recommended changes include editing the logical names that WinRunner provides for these items. In my opinion, this makes it a better choice. But it is also slower.

As shown in Figure 16.5, I have selected the Express mode for this book. Use this mode if you are new to this wizard or doing casual testing. This mode is considerably faster. Now, we are ready to have the wizard create the GUI Map. Click Learn and just sit back.

The RapidTest Script Wizard now begins to walk through the entire application. As it does so it opens up each of the windows in the AUT, learns the object and repeats the process on the next window. You may be asked to show the tool how to perform a certain operation such as closing a window, if the wizard gets stuck in a process. The entire process is exceedingly fast, and on completion, the dialog in Figure 16.6 is displayed.

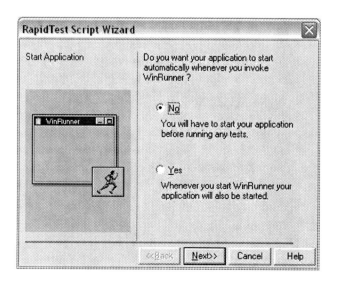

Figure 16.6: The Start Application page.

This dialog asks if you want WinRunner to automatically launch your AUT whenever WinRunner is launched. I typically enter No in this screen because I test a variety of applications and having my AUT pop-up every time I run WinRunner would be a nuisance. Click Next.

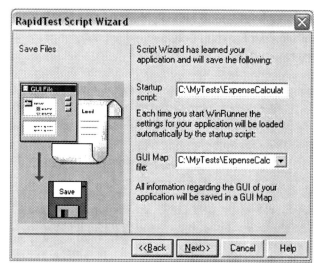

Figure 16.7: The Save Files page.

In the dialog shown in Figure 16.7, WinRunner requests you to enter 2 pieces of information.

Startup Script - The name and location of a script that will be executed whenever WinRunner is started. This script contains relevant functions for running the tests created by WinRunner. Listing 16.1 shows the contents of this startup script.

The GUI Map File name - This is the name that the GUI Map file should be saved as and the location on the filesystem for the file.

```
GUI_load("C:\\MyTests\\ExpenseCalculatorRapidTest.GUI")
```

Listing 16.1: The startup script created.

An additional dialog is also displayed prompting you for a name for each of the tests you instructed the wizard to create.

Click Next from this dialog and the dialog shown in Figure 16.8 is displayed. This dialog merely congratulates you for successfully using the RapidTest Script Wizard for your testing needs.

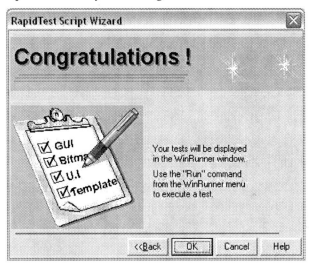

Figure 16.8: The Congratulations page.

Congratulations indeed! You have successfully used the RapidTest Script Wizard. Now that the tests are created, you will notice that several tests have been added to your test window. Listing 16.2 shows the test template that was created by the wizard.

```
time_out=getvar("timeout");
win_open("Expense Calculator - (Default)",time_out);
#Enter code for window "Expense Calculator - (Default)" here

win_open("About Expense Calculator",time_out);
```

171

```
#Enter code for window "About Expense Calculator" here

type("<kEsc>");
win_open("Expense Summary",time_out);
#Enter code for window "Expense Summary" here


win_close("Expense Summary");
win_open("New Account",time_out);
#Enter code for window "New Account" here

win_close("New Account");
win_open("Open Account",time_out);
#Enter code for window "Open Account" here

win_close("Open Account");
```

Listing 16.2: The test template create for Expense Calculator.

Notice that all the test template does is open your AUT's windows by using the win_open function. It also closes these windows after use using the win_close function. For your tests, you could choose to record your actions into this TSL test template. Don't forget to remove sections that are irrelevant to your current test case.

STARTUP SCRIPTS

Whenever WinRunner is launched, it executes a script file that sets certain variables and performs some operations. This script file is named **tslinit** and is found with the **dat** folder of the WinRunner installation.

Unless you are a WinRunner expert, it is not advisable to edit this script. If you want additional operations to be performed by WinRunner at startup, you should create your own WinRunner script and specify this as the WinRunner startup test. WinRunner will execute this on startup after executing the **tslinit** script.

To inform WinRunner to run your script, navigate to Tools ▶ General Options ▶ General ▶ Startup and specify your test script in the startup test field.

Repeating the RapidTest Script Wizard

If you launch the RapidTest Script Wizard to create scripts for a application that already has a GUI Map file created and loaded into WinRunner, WinRunner immediately detects this and generates a different screen to verify what you want to do.

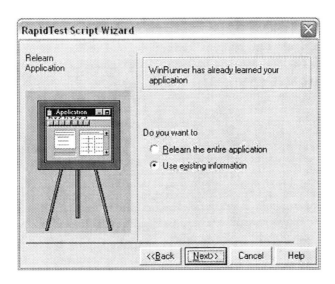

Figure 16.9: The Relearn Application page.

Shown in Figure 16.9, this screen informs you that the objects in your application are already known to WinRunner and prompts you to choose one of the following actions:

Relearn the entire application – create a new GUI Map for the application and use this for all tests.

Use existing information – use existing information from the loaded GUI Map file to create the tests.

Summary

In this chapter you have learned:

- What the RapidTest Script Wizard is and how to use it.

- The different items that can be created by the RapidTest Script Wizard and what they are used for.

- How to set a startup test in WinRunner to run whenever you launch the tool.

APPENDIX A

GLOSSARY OF TERMS

A

acceptance testing – Testing by the client before accepting delivery of the AUT. The testing is done to ensure that the functional, usability and performance requirements of the system have been met.

accessibility testing – Testing to ensure that the AUT is easy for use with for users with disabilities.

actual result – The observed value/information captured when the AUT is being tested.

ad-hoc testing –An unstructured form of testing where functionality is tested for based on the biases of the tester. It is often used to quickly test a specific functionality.

availability –The degree to which the AUT is operational and accessible when required for use. This is often expressed as a percentage.

Application Under Test (AUT) – Used to refer to the application being tested instead of having to repeatedly specify the name of the application.

AUT – Abbreviation for Application Under Test.

automated testing – Software testing using automated testing tools. This involves the use of tools to create an automated testing script which can then later be executed in a unattended state.

B

back-to-back testing – Testing in which two or more variants of a component or system are executed with the same inputs, the outputs compared, and analyzed in cases of discrepancies.

baseline – A specification or software product that has been formally reviewed or agreed upon, that thereafter serves as the basis for further development, and that can be changed only through a formal change control process.

behavior – The response of a component or system to a set of input values and preconditions.

benchmark test – A standard against which measurements or comparisons can be made.

beta testing – Operational testing by potential and/or existing users/customers at an external site not otherwise involved with the developers, to determine whether the AUT meets with requirements.

black box testing – Testing a system by providing input and examining output without knowledge and/or regard of the internal code of the system.

bottom-up testing: An incremental approach to integration testing where the lowest level components are tested first, and then used to facilitate the testing of higher level components. This process is repeated until the component at the top of the hierarchy is tested. See also integration testing.

business process – a series of steps defined in a business requirement, which when sequentially executed, performs a complete business function.

C

checkpoint – Code statements used to check that a certain point, in the execution of a test, an item has a certain predetermined value. This helps to determine correctness of the application.

Capability Maturity Model (CMM) – A five level staged framework that describes the key elements of an effective software process. The Capability Maturity Model covers practices for planning, engineering and managing software development and maintenance.

complexity – The degree to which a component or system has a design and/or internal structure that is difficult to understand, maintain and verify.

condition – A logical expression that can be evaluated as True or False, e.g. 3 > 2.

context menu – A pop–up menu that is triggered by a left or right click.

D

data table - An object that encapsulates a spreadsheet in QTP allowing a test to be configured and execute with dynamic data. The data table object allows us to interact with an Excel spreadsheet in which we store configuration information for our test.

data driven testing – A scripting technique that stores test input and expected results in a table or spreadsheet, so that a single control script can execute all of the tests in the table. Data driven testing is often used with automated testing tools such as WinRunner.

debugging – The process of finding, analyzing and removing the causes of failures in software.

decision – A program point at which the control flow has two or more alternative routes. A node with two or more links to separate branches.

defect – A flaw in a component or system that can cause the component or system to fail to perform its required function, e.g. an incorrect statement or data definition. A defect, if encountered during execution, may cause a failure of the component or system.

defect report – A document reporting on any flaw in a component or system that can cause the component or system to fail to perform its required function.

defect management – The process of recognizing, investigating, taking action and disposing of defects. It involves recording defects, classifying them and identifying the impact.

deliverable – A work product that has to delivered as part of completion of the project.

dynamic testing – Testing that involves the execution of the software of a component or system.

E

emulator - A device, computer program, or system that accepts the same inputs and produces the same outputs as a given system.

exception handling – Handling of popup messages that are not part of the test objective and may interfere with the progress of the test.

expected result - The behavior predicted by the specification, or another source, of the component or system under specified conditions.

F

fail - A test is deemed to fail if its actual result does not match its expected result.

feature - An attribute of a component or system specified or implied by requirements documentation.

function - modular units of functionality that make up a test. Functions can be built-in or user created.

functional requirement - A requirement that specifies a function that a component or system must perform.

functional testing - Testing based on an analysis of the specification of the functionality of a component or system. This testing is often done from the user perspective. See black box testing.

functionality - The capability of the software product to provide functions which meet stated and implied needs when the software is used under specified conditions.

G

GUI Map Editor – A tool that is used to create/edit the object mapping file known as the GUI Map.

GUI Spy - A tool that provides a real–time listing of all the property/value pairs of a chosen object.

I

incident – Any event occurring during testing that requires investigation.

integration testing – Testing performed to expose defects in the interfaces and in the interactions between integrated components or systems.

interoperability – The capability of the software product to interact with one or more specified components or systems.

K

keyword driven testing – A scripting technique that uses data files to contain not only test data and expected results, but also keywords related to the application being tested. The keywords are interpreted by special supporting scripts that are called by the control script for the test.

L

load test – A test type concerned with measuring the behavior of a component or system with increasing load, e.g. number of parallel users and/or numbers of transactions to determine what load can be handled by the component or system.

P

pointing – The process employed by multiple WinRunner tools that requires you to click on a hand icon and then click on the object you wish to point to. This allows WinRunner to capture information about the object you want to select.

M

maintenance – Modification of a software product after delivery to correct defects, to improve performance or other attributes, or to adapt the product to a modified environment.

maintainability – The ease with which a software product can be modified to correct defects, modified to meet new requirements, modified to make future maintenance easier, or adapted to a changed environment.

measurement – The process of assigning a number or category to an entity to describe an attribute of that entity.

metric – A measurement scale and the method used for measurement.

milestone – A point in time in a project at which defined (intermediate) deliverables and results should be ready.

monitor – A software tool or hardware device that run concurrently with the component or system under test and supervises, records and/or analyses the behavior of the component or system.

N

negative testing – Tests aimed at showing that a component or system does not work. Often involves feeding the system with invalid input/operations to see if the system accepts it.

non-functional requirement – A requirement that does not relate to functionality, but to attributes of such as reliability, efficiency, usability, maintainability and portability.

non-functional testing – Testing the attributes of the AUT based on its non-functional requirements.

O

object – Items in the user interface of an application such as buttons, edit fields, input fields, list boxes, combo boxes etc.

operational environment – Hardware and software products installed at users' or customers' sites where the component or system under test will be used. The software may include operating systems, database management systems, and other applications.

operational testing – Testing conducted to evaluate a component or system in its operational environment.

Q

quality – The degree to which the AUT meets specified requirements and/or user/customer needs and expectations.

quality assurance – Part of quality management focused on providing confidence that quality requirements will be fulfilled.

quality management – Coordinated activities to direct and control an organization with regard to quality. It includes the establishment of the quality policy and quality objectives, quality planning, quality control, quality assurance and quality improvement.

P

parameterization - the process of replacing hard-coded values within a test with references to the data table.

pass - A test is deemed to pass if its actual result matches its expected result.

pass/fail criteria - Decision rules used to determine whether a test item (function) or feature has passed or failed a test.

performance - The degree to which a system or component accomplishes its designated functions within given constraints regarding processing time and throughput rate.

portability - The ease with which the software product can be transferred from one hardware or software environment to another.

post-condition - Environmental and state conditions that must be fulfilled after the execution of a test or test procedure.

pre-condition - Environmental and state conditions that must be fulfilled before the component or system can be executed with a particular test or test procedure.

priority - The level of (business) importance assigned to an item, e.g. defect.

process – A set of interrelated activities, which transform inputs into outputs.

Q

quality assurance – Part of quality management focused on providing confidence that quality requirements will be fulfilled.

quality management – Coordinated activities to direct and control an organization with regard to quality. Direction and control with regard to quality generally includes the establishment of the quality policy and quality objectives, quality planning, quality control, quality assurance and quality improvement.

R

record/playback tool – A type of test execution tool where inputs are recorded during manual testing in order to generate automated test scripts that can be executed later (i.e. replayed). WinRunner is an example of such a tool.

regression testing – Testing of a previously tested program following modification to ensure that defects have not been introduced or uncovered in unchanged areas of the software, as a result of the changes made.

reliability – The ability of the software product to perform its required functions under stated conditions for a specified period of time, or for a specified number of operations.

requirement – A condition or capability needed by a user to solve a problem or achieve an objective that must be met or possessed by a system or system component to satisfy a contract, standard, specification, or other formally imposed document.

requirements phase – The period of time in the software life cycle during which the requirements for a software product are defined and documented.

result – The consequence/outcome of the execution of a test. It includes outputs to screens, changes to data, reports, and communication messages sent out. See also actual result, expected result.

review – An evaluation of a project status to ascertain discrepancies from planned results and to recommend improvements.

risk – A factor that could result in future negative consequences; usually expressed as impact and likelihood.

risk analysis – The process of assessing identified risks to estimate their impact and likelihood of occurrence.

robustness – The degree to which a component or system can function correctly in the presence of invalid inputs or stressful environmental conditions.

S

sanity test – This type of testing is also called sanity testing and is done in order to check if the application is ready for further major testing and is working properly without failing up to least expected level.

scalability – The capability of the software product to be upgraded to accommodate increased loads.

scripting language – A programming language in which executable test scripts are written, used by a test execution tool.

security testing – Testing the application from a security perspective to ensure that users can do everything, and only everything, that they have been given the access rights to do.

severity – The degree of impact that a defect has on the development or operation of a component or system.

simulation – The representation of selected behavioral characteristics of one physical or abstract system by another system.

smoke testing – Testing the application in order to ensure that the current build of the application/system is sufficiently stable for further, more comprehensive, testing to be performed. A daily build and smoke test is among industry best practices.

software quality – The totality of functionality and features of a software product that bear on its ability to satisfy stated or implied needs.

specification – A document that specifies, ideally in a complete, precise and verifiable manner, the requirements, design, behavior, or other characteristics of a component or system, and, often, the procedures for determining whether these provisions have been satisfied.

stability – The capability of the software product to avoid unexpected effects from modifications in the software.

state diagram – A diagram that depicts the states that a component or system can assume, and shows the events or circumstances that cause and/or result from a change from one state to another.

statement – An entity in a programming language, which is typically the smallest indivisible unit of execution.

stress testing – This involves placing the system at maximum load for an extended period of time to monitor its performance under stress.

system testing – Testing that takes place when all the modular units that make up a software system have been fully integrated. Therefore, system testing happens way after integration testing.

System Under Test (SUT) – Similar to AUT, but used when the item being tested is not an application but a hardware device, or business process.

T

test – A set of one or more test cases.

test automation – The use of software to perform or support test activities, e.g. test management, test design, test execution and results checking.

test case – A set of input values, execution pre-conditions, expected results and execution post-conditions, developed for a particular objective or test condition, such as to exercise a particular program path or to verify compliance with a specific requirement.

test case specification – A document specifying a set of test cases (objective, inputs, test actions, expected results, and execution preconditions) for a test item.

test condition – An item or event of a component or system that could be verified by one or more test cases, e.g. a function, transaction, quality attribute, or structural element.

test data – Data that exists (for example, in a database) before a test is executed, and that affects or is affected by the component or system under test.

test execution – The process of running a test by the component or system under test, producing actual result(s).

test execution technique – The method used to perform the actual test execution, either manually or automated.

test item – The individual element to be tested. There usually is one test object and many test items.

test management – The planning, estimating, monitoring and control of test activities, typically carried out by a test manager.

test phase – A distinct set of test activities collected into a manageable phase of a project, e.g. the execution activities of a test level.

test plan – A document containing the entire details of how to test an application including all necessary specifications, standards, test cases, and any other necessary information useful in testing the application.

test scenario – Describes the process for fully testing a business process of the AUT. A Test Scenario may be comprised of several test cases.

test script – Commonly used to refer to a test procedure specification, especially an automated one.

test suite – A set of several test cases for a component or system under test, where the post condition of one test is often used as the precondition for the next one.

test tool – A software product that supports one or more test activities, such as planning and control, specification, building initial files and data, test execution and test analysis.

test type – A group of test activities aimed at testing a component or system regarding one or more interrelated quality attributes. A test type is focused on a specific test objective, i.e. reliability test, usability test, regression test etc., and may take place on one or more test levels or test phases.

Test Script Language (TSL) – The C-like script language used by WinRunner for specifying the operations which would be performed in the test.

testability – The capability of the software product to enable modified software to be tested.

testing – The process consisting of all life cycle activities, both static and dynamic, concerned with planning, preparation and evaluation of software products and related work products to determine that they satisfy specified requirements, to demonstrate that they are fit for purpose and to detect defects.

traceability – The ability to identify related items in documentation and software, such as requirements with associated tests.

U

user interface testing – Testing the user interface application to help ensure that it is user friendly and (optionally) meets with standard software accessibility guidelines.

unit testing – This form is done by developers as it involves testing the individual component of a software system. This is loosely defined enough to be interpreted as anything from a function to a class.

usability – The capability of the software to be understood, learned, used and attractive to the user when used under specified conditions.

user test – A test whereby real-life users are involved to evaluate the usability of a component or system.

V

validation – Confirmation by examination and through provision of objective evidence that the requirements for a specific intended use or application have been fulfilled.

variable – An element of storage in a computer that is accessible by a software program by referring to it by a name.

verification – Confirmation by examination and through the provision of objective evidence that specified requirements have been fulfilled.

W

white box testing – Testing based on an analysis of the internal structure of the component or system.

Several items from this glossary are based on the document *Glossary of terms used in Software Testing* created by the *Glossary Working Party* of the *International Software Testing Qualification Board*. Many thanks are due to all the contributors to the excellent document.

APPENDIX B

EXPENSE CALCULATOR TEST CASES

We have created some tests in this book, and in this appendix section, I have included several additional test cases that can be used in testing our AUT. You can use these tests to practice the creation of WinRunner test scripts.

Test Name:
    Delete Expense

Purpose:
    Verify that expenses are deleted from the display grid when a delete operation is invoked.

Pre-Conditon:
    There are more than two existing expenses in the account before this test is executed.

Step	User Action	Expected Result
1	Launch the AUT	
2	Select the first expense in the grid and delete it by clicking Actions -> Delete in the menu	Number of expenses in the expense grid is reduced by 1.
3	Select the first expense in the grid and delete it by pressing the Delete key	Number of expenses in the expense grid is reduced by 1.
4	Close the AUT	

```
Post-Condition:
    None

Valid Test Data:
    N/A
```

Listing B.1: Delete Expense Test Case.

```
Test Name:
    Check Navigation

Purpose:
    Verify that all windows in the application are
    displayed when the appropriate menu operations are
    invoked.

Pre-Conditon:
    None.
```

Step	User Action	Expected Result
1	Launch the AUT	Main window is displayed.
2	Invoke the New Accounts dialog by clicking File -> New Account from the menu	New Account dialog is displayed
3	Close the dialog by clicking the Cancel button	
4	Invoke the Open Accounts dialog by clicking File -> Open Account from the menu	Open Account dialog is displayed
5	Close the dialog by clicking the Cancel button	
6	Invoke the Summary dialog by clicking Actions -> View Summary from the	Summary dialog is displayed

Step	User Action	Expected Result
	menu	
7	Close the dialog by clicking the Close button	
8	Invoke the About dialog by clicking Help -> About from the menu	About dialog is displayed
9	Close the dialog by clicking the Ok button	
10	Close the AUT	

Post-Condition:
    None

Valid Test Data:
    N/A

Listing B.2: Check Navigation Test Case.

Test Name:
    Check App Details

Purpose:
    Verify default settings in the application match
    the defaults specified in the requirements.

Pre-Conditon:
    None.

Step	User Action	Expected Result
1	Launch the AUT	The following default values are included: a. Todays Date button has focus b. Save button is the default button c. Totals textbox is read only
2	Invoke the About	Application shows

Step	User Action	Expected Result
	dialog by clicking Help -> About from the menu	version 1.0.* (* reflects the build number and is not checked)
3	Close the dialog by clicking the Ok button	
4	Close the AUT	

Post-Condition:
> None

Valid Test Data:
> N/A

Listing B.3: Check App Details Test Case.

Test Name:
> View Summary

Purpose:
> Verify that the Summary window is displayed on invocation.

Pre-Conditon:
> The account displayed contains more than one expense.

Step	User Action	Expected Result
1	Launch the AUT	
2	Invoke the Summary dialog by clicking Actions -> View Summary from the menu	Summary dialog is displayed
3	Close the dialog by clicking the Close button	
4	Close the AUT	

Post-Condition:
> None

Valid Test Data:
      N/A

Listing B.4: View Summary Test Case.

Test Name:
      View System Info

Purpose:
      Ensure that the Window's System Info application
      is successfully launched.

Pre-Conditon:
      None

Step	User Action	Expected Result
1	Launch the AUT	
2	Invoke the About dialog by clicking Help -> About from the menu	About dialog is displayed
3	Click the System Info button	The Windows System Info application is executed
4	Close the About dialog by clicking the Ok button	
5	Close the AUT	
6	Close the System Info application	

Post-Condition:
      None

Valid Test Data:
      N/A

Listing B.5: View System Info Test Case.

Test Name:

Verify Total

Purpose:

Ensure that the amount displayed in the total's textbox is the correct sum of expenses displayed in the amount column of the grid. The total should also be displayed in $#,###.00 (currency) format.

Pre-Conditon:

The account displayed contains more than three expenses totalling over $1000 in amount.

Step	User Action	Expected Result
1	Launch the AUT	The amount shown in the totals textbox is the sum of amounts shown in the Amount column of the grid. This value must be in $#,###.00 format.
2	Close the System Info application	

Post-Condition:

None

Valid Test Data:

N/A

Listing B.6: Verify Totals Test Case.

Test Name:

Verify Required Fields

Purpose:

Ensure that expenses cannot be saved with any of the required fields missing.

Pre-Conditon:

None

Step	User Action	Expected Result
1	Launch the AUT	
2	Click the Save button	Error message is displayed stating that the date is missing
3	Close the error message dialog	Cursor focus is on the date field
4	Click the Today's Date button and click the Save button	Error message is displayed stating that the description is missing
5	Close the error message dialog	Cursor focus is on the description field
6	Enter a description and click the Save button	Error message is displayed stating that the category is missing
7	Close the error message dialog	Cursor focus is on the category field
8	Choose a category and click the Save button	Error message is displayed stating that the amount is missing
9	Close the error message dialog	Cursor focus is on the amount field
10	Enter a valid amount and click the Save button	Expense is saved to the database and displayed in the grid
11	Close the AUT	

Post-Condition:
    None

Valid Test Data:
    None

Listing B.7: Verify Required Fields Test Case.

Test Name:
    Ensure Valid Date

Purpose:
    Ensure that expenses cannot be saved using an
    invalid date.

Pre-Conditon:
    None

Step	User Action	Expected Result
1	Launch the AUT	
2	Type in an expense using data from below and click the Save button	Error message is displayed stating that the date is invalid
3	Close the error message dialog	Cursor focus is on the date field
4	Click the Today's date button and click the Save button	Expense is saved to the database and displayed in the grid
5	Close the AUT	

Post-Condition:
    None

Valid Test Data:
    Date: <invalid date e.g. 13/32/07>
    Description: Venti non-fat no-whip ice mocha
    Category: Snacks
    Amount: 23.45

Listing B.8: Ensure Valid Date Test Case.

Test Name:
    Ensure Valid Amount

Purpose:
    Ensure that expenses cannot be saved using an
    invalid amount.

Pre-Conditon:
    None

Step	User Action	Expected Result
1	Launch the AUT	
2	Type in an expense using data from below and click the Save button	Error message is displayed stating that the amount is invalid
3	Close the error message dialog	Cursor focus is on the amount field
4	Enter a valid amount and click the Save button	Expense is saved to the database and displayed in the grid
5	Close the AUT	

Post-Condition:
    None

Valid Test Data:
    Date: 1/1/2007
    Description: Venti non-fat no-whip ice mocha
    Category: Snacks
    Amount: <invalid amount e.g. 2.bc>

Listing B.9: Ensure Valid Amount Test Case.

Test Name:
    Verify Exit

Purpose:
    Verify that the application closes when terminated using the close button or the menu.

Pre-Conditon:
    None

Step	User Action	Expected Result
1	Launch the AUT	
2	Close the AUT by clicking on the Close button on the title bar	Application exits
3	Launch the AUT	

| 4 | Close the AUT using the menu by clicking File -> Exit | Application exits |

Post-Condition:
    None

Valid Test Data:
    None

Listing B.10: Verify Exit Test Case.

Test Name:
    Grid vs DB

Purpose:
    Verify that the grid displays the correct number
    of database records for the given account.

Pre-Conditon:
    None

Step	User Action	Expected Result
1	Launch the AUT	Grid count matches the number of records in the database for the default account
2	Close the AUT	Application exits

Post-Condition:
    None

Valid Test Data:
    None

Listing B.11: Grid vs. DB Test Case.

Test Name:
    New Account

Purpose:

    Ensure that when a new account is opened, the
    correct defaults are set.

Pre-Conditon:

    None

Step	User Action	Expected Result
1	Launch the AUT	
2	Click on File->New Account	The New Account dialog is displayed
3	Enter a new account name	
4	Click the Ok button	a. Main window caption contains account name b. Grid shows no records c. Total's textbox has a value of $0.00
5	Close the AUT	Application exits

Post-Condition:

    None

Valid Test Data:

    Account name that doesn't exist. Use the SQL code
    below to identify existing accounts:
    SELECT DISTINCT ACCOUNT FROM EXPENSES

Listing B.12: New Account Test Case.

Test Name:

    Open Account

Purpose:

    Ensure that when an existing account is reopened,
    the correct defaults are set.

Pre-Conditon:

    More than one account exists

Step	User Action	Expected Result
1	Launch the AUT	
2	Click on File->Open Account	The Open Account dialog is displayed
3	Select an existing account from the drop down list	
4	Click the Ok button	a. Main window caption contains account name
5	Close the AUT	Application exits

Post-Condition:
    None

Valid Test Data:
    None

Listing B.13: Open Account Test Case.

Test Name:
    Verify Mnemonics

Purpose:
    Ensure that all command shortcuts work properly.

Pre-Conditon:
    Account dialog contains more than one account

Step	User Action	Expected Result
1	Launch the AUT	Main window is displayed.
2	Invoke the New Accounts dialog by pressing Ctrl+N	New Account dialog is displayed
3	Close the dialog by clicking the Cancel button	
4	Invoke the Open Accounts dialog by pressing Ctrl+O	Open Account dialog is displayed

5	Close the dialog by clicking the Cancel button	
6	Select the first record in the grid and press the Delete key	Number of expenses in the expense grid is reduced by 1
7	Press Alt+T	The correct system date is entered in the date textbox
8	Enter a valid expense	
9	Save the expense by pressing Alt+S	Number of expenses in the expense grid is increased by 1
10	Close the AUT by pressing Shift+F4	Application closes

Post-Condition:
      None

Valid Test Data:
      Description: Chocolate chip cookie dough
      Category: Snacks
      Amount: 4.55

Listing B.14: Verify Mnemonics Test Case.

APPENDIX C

TSL vs. VBScript

Throughout this book, I have tried to increase your expertise with TSL, the script language used by WinRunner. You may already be familiar with another of Mercury's offerings, QuickTest Professional (QTP). QTP is targeted for use by programmers and non-programmers alike and it supports some of the newer and emerging technologies such as Flash, .Net and other technologies.

In this appendix, I provide a high level comparison between the scripting languages used in WinRunner and in QTP. It is often said that the most difficult programming language to master is your first programming (or script) language, after that, all other languages merely involve some differing syntax rules and minor additions/deletions in the constructs available to the script language.

By now, you know that TSL is the built-in language in WinRunner, for QTP, the comparable language is VBScript. Both TSL and VBScript provide generally the same set of functionality to their host automated testing tools. The languages allow the respective tools to manipulate their system environment, replay user operations, and verify certain details within the application. It is important to remember that both QTP and WinRunner provide similar test automation functionality.

Depending on the Mercury tool you are using for your automated testing, you need to write either TSL or VBScript. For this appendix section to be useful to you, you should already know how to write either VBScript or WinRunner. It is also fine if you know how to write some other language. What is presented below is a comparison of the two languages including syntax, keywords, operators, and expressions etc.

NOTE: This is a comparison of TSL to VBScript and NOT a comparison of WinRunner to QTP.

So, for example, there will be no reference to Actions or Compiled Modules etc. in this text since those are artifacts of WinRunner and QTP respectively but not contents of the TSL or VBScript languages.

The comparison of the two languages is laid out in the following sections.
- Historical context
- Advantages of each language
- Keyword Differences
- Operator Differences
- Programmatic differences

Historical context

This section delves into a bit of the history behind each of the languages.

TSL	VBScript
Based on the C family of languages and so has similarities to JavaScript, Perl, Java etc.	Belongs to the Visual Basic family of languages and is therefore related to VB, VBA and VB.NET.
Owned by Mercury Interactive and used in their WinRunner, XRunner (defunct) and LoadRunner tools.	Owned by Microsoft and licensed for usage in many tools and software products.
Procedural language with heavy reliance on functions.	Used as an industry standard language for web developments, Windows's scripting, and as a macro language.

Advantages of each language

What are the useful features that exist in each of these languages?

TSL	VBScript
Very compact with a reliance on symbols.	Simple and uses English-like keywords instead of symbols.
Supports the use of Dynamic Link Libraries (DLL) thereby using complex functionality from more powerful languages.	Supports the creation of COM objects and therefore advanced interaction with the system shell.
Supports the use of operator overloading, though this advanced concepts should be left to experts.	Can use the With syntax to make object hierarchy easier to understand.
	Supports object notation and therefore

	object manipulation.
	Can force explicit declaration using the Option Explicit.

Keyword Differences

Difference in the keywords that exist in the languages

Purpose	TSL	VB.NET
Comments	`#`	`'`
		`Rem`
Declare a variable	`static [Test]`	`Dim`
	`auto [Function]`	
Declare a constant	`const`	`Const`
Force explicit declaration of variables	`n/a`	`Option Explicit`
If	`if (condition) {`	`If (condition) Then`
	`    some statements;`	`    Some statements`
	`}`	`End If`
If...Else	`if (condition) {`	`If (condition) Then`
	`    some statements;`	`    Some statements`
	`}`	`Else`
	`else {`	`    Some statements`
	`    some statements;`	`End If`
	`}`	
If...ElseIf...Else	`if (condition) {`	`If (condition) Then`
	`    some statements;`	`    Some statements`
	`}`	`ElseIf (condition) Then`
	`else if (condition) {`	`    Some statements`
	`    some statements;`	`Else`
	`}`	`    Some statements`
	`else {`	`End If`
	`    some statements;`	
	`}`	
Select Case/switch	`switch (variable) {`	`Select Case variable`
	`    case value1: some`	

	`statements;`	Case *value1*
	`break;`	`some statements`
	`case value2: some` `statements;`	Case *value2*
		`some statements`
	`break;`	Case Else
	`default: some` `statements;`	`some statements`
	`}`	End Select
While Loop	`while(condition) {`	While (*condition*)
	`some statements;`	`some code`
	`}`	While
Do…While Loop	`do {`	Do
	`some statements;`	`some code`
	`} while(condition);`	Loop While (*condition*)
Do…Until Loop	`N/A`	Do
		`some code`
		Loop Until (*condition*)
For Loop	`for(initialize;` `condition; modify) {`	For *var* = *start* To *finish* Step *number*
	`some statements;`	`some code`
	`[continue;]`	`[Exit For]`
	`}`	Next
For Each Loop	`for (x in list) {`	For Each *x* In *list*
	`some statements;`	`some statements`
	`}`	Next
Function with a return value	`function myFunction()`	Function myFunction()
	`some statements;`	`some statements`
	`return value;`	`myFunction = some value`
	`}`	End Function
Function without a return value	`function myFunction()`	Sub mySub()
	`some statements;`	`some statements`
	`}`	End Sub

Operator Differences

Difference in the operators that exist in the languages

Purpose	Category	TSL	VBScript
Addition	Arithmetic	+	+
Subtract	Arithmetic	−	−
Division	Arithmetic	/	/
Integer Division	Arithmetic	n/a	\
Multiplication	Arithmetic	*	*
Exponent	Arithmetic	^ or **	^
Modulo	Arithmetic	%	/
Increment	Arithmetic	++	n/a
Decrement	Arithmetic	--	n/a
Assignment	Assignment	=	=
Concatenation	Concatenation	&	&
Conjunction	Logical	&&	And
Disjunction	Logical	||	Or
Negation	Logical	!	Not
Exclusivity	Logical	n/a	Xor
More Than	Comparison	>	>
Less Than	Comparison	<	<
More Than Or Equals	Comparison	>=	>=
Less Than Or Equals	Comparison	<=	<=
Equals	Comparison	==	=
Not Equal	Comparison	!=	<>

Programmatic differences

Difference in the coding of each language.

Purpose	TSL	VBScript
Object notation	Not supported	Supported
Syntax	Terse and symbol based. Considered rather cryptic by	English-like with a reliance on words

	some	
Variable declaration	Implicit. But in functions, all variables must be declared.	Implicit. But the Option Explicit directive can be used to force explicit declaration.
Case Sensitivity	Case sensitive	Not case sensitive
Data-typing	Loosely typed.	Loosely typed. Supports many internal datatypes but they are resolve to the Variant type.
Script language type	Interpreted	Interpreted

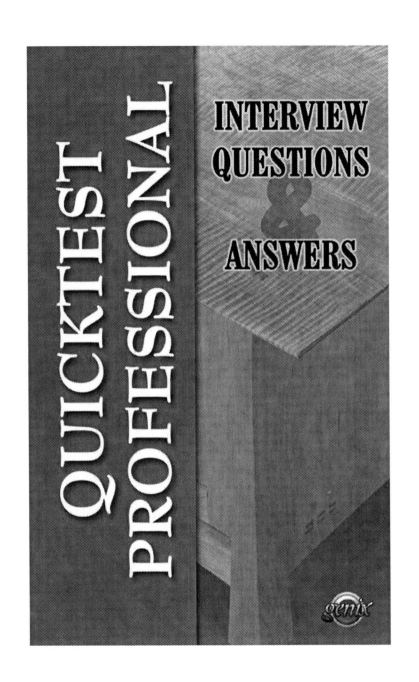

AVAILABLE IN OCTOBER '07

Printed in the United States
143619LV00001B/65/A

9 780615 152899